ON

Great ideas for improving your life and your business from some of America's top speakers, trainers, consultants, and authors.

LARRY WINGET • SAM SILVERSTEIN • KEITH HARRELL
ROXANNE EMMERICH • MARC HARDY • SCOTT MCKAIN
LISA FORD • VIC OSTEEN • DAN CLARK • SHEP HYKEN

Only The Best

ON

Leadership

compiled by
Larry Winget

Printed in the United States Of America.

Cover design and layout by Ad Graphics, Tulsa, Oklahoma.

Library of congress Catalog Number: 96-061320

ISBN:1-881342-15-8

"Only The Best ™" is a trademark of Win Publications!, Win Seminars!, and Larry Winget, denoting a series of books and other products that may include but is not limited to pocket cards, calendars, audio cassettes and videotapes.

Published by:

Win Publications!
a subsidiary of Win Seminars!, Inc.
P. O. Box 700485
Tulsa, Oklahoma 74170
918 745-6606

Additional copies of
Only The Best On Leadership
can be obtained from any of the authors by calling their individual number as listed with their chapter.

Quantity discounts are available.

All of the authors represented in
Only The Best On Leadership
are members of the
National Speakers Association.

If you have an upcoming meeting and need a great speaker or even several great speakers then this book represents some of the finest in the business. Any of them would do an excellent job presenting an informative, entertaining keynote or seminar.

Please contact any speaker to recieve a full packet of materials explaining their speaking services and other products that may be available.

Contents

ON

CUSTOMER SERVICE

Great ideas for improving your life and your business from some of America's top speakers, trainers, consultants, and authors.

SHEP HYKEN • SUE HERSHKOWITZ • KEITH HARRELL • MIKKI WILLIAMS
DAN CLARK • VIC OSTEEN • SCOTT MCKAIN • LISA FORD • MEL KLEIMAN
ROXANNE EMMERICH • SUE PISTONE • MARC HARDY • LARRY WINGET

To order,
contact any of the authors
or call
800 749-4597

1

Only The BEST

Leadership Lessons From My Television Heroes

By

Larry Winget

Leadership Lessons From My Television Heroes

Larry Winget

First of all, let me say you are right! I did watch too much television when I was growing up. But when I was a boy, television was full of role models, or for me, heroes. I loved Tarzan, Superman, Sergeant Preston of the Yukon, and The Lone Ranger. As I grew older, I called upon the stories of my television heroes to inspire me. I also recalled some of the things they did and said to remind me of what they would do when faced with a situation similar to my own.

For instance, think of my hero, Tarzan. Tarzan quickly learned that by comparison to the other creatures of the jungle, he was ill-equipped to survive in the jungle. He was frail by comparison to his ape family. He was slow compared to the antelope, small compared to the elephant, and couldn't climb a tree nearly as well as his chimpanzee friend, Cheetah. I am sure that he questioned his ability to survive. He obviously was quick to learn the Law of the Jungle — Survival Of The Fittest. He learned that you have to be bigger, stronger, faster, or smarter to survive. Otherwise, you're lunch. Now Tarzan was not bigger or stronger or even faster than most of the animals. So he used the one thing that made him different, his intellect. He didn't waste much time focusing on his weaknesses; instead he focused on his unique strength. As leaders, we have to do the same thing. We have to understand the Law of the Jungle, survival. And if we pay attention, we will notice that it is not always the biggest, the strongest, the fastest who make it in business. It is usually the smartest.

Lesson Number One

We must identify our strength, develop it and use it to survive.

Tarzan was a man of very few words. In fact, he really only had one word. It was "Ungawa." But it was a good word. Tarzan could be in any situation and when he said Ungawa, we all knew what he was talking about. Instead of a man of words, Tarzan was a man of action.

Lesson Number Two

Talk less, do more.

Tarzan was a well balanced human being. He slept when he was sleepy. We often saw him napping in a tree even in the middle of the day. He ate when he was hungry, and it was definitely a healthy diet with lots of fresh fruit and vegetables. He exercised regularly. In fact, he often walked to work. He took time to play. We often saw Tarzan frolicking in the water or playing with Cheetah or taking a casual drive through the jungle on Simba, the elephant. He loved animals and had a pet who was his best friend. He was a family man who had a wife, Jane, and later even adopted an orphan and named him Boy. Creative name, huh?

Lesson Number Three
Live a simple, balanced life.

Look! Up in the sky, it's a bird. It's a plane. No, it's Superman!

What a guy. A glasses-wearing geek with a day job. Somehow I can identify with that. But then, in a time of crisis he would duck into a phone booth (he would have a hard time doing that today — seen any phone booths lately?) and change into Superman! He was ready to face any foe, any challenger, anyone who threatened Truth, Justice, and the American Way! I loved this guy. But you know what I liked the most about Superman? It didn't matter who he was being at the time, Superman or Clark Kent, he always kept his cool. He really was mild mannered. We never saw him lose him temper, scream at anyone, deck anyone out of anger, or belittle anyone because of their mistakes.

I don't see much of that today. I see people lose their tempers, scream at their employees, belittle them for making a mistake and lash out at competitors in anger. We have come to the point where we think that signs of aggression show our power, but they really only reveal our weakness. Power is when we remain calm under pressure, not when we lose control. What a great lesson for leaders today.

Lesson Number Four

True power comes from remaining calm and in control while under pressure.

However, regardless of the fact that Superman was the most powerful being on the planet, he had a weakness, something that could kill him . . . Kryptonite! Therefore, he was constantly on guard against becoming exposed to it. We all have our weaknesses. We are all vulnerable. Our Kryptonite isn't a green rock from another planet. It usually takes on other disguises. It may be a tolerance for mediocrity, the inability to make a decision, a lack of vision, laziness, or many other things. In order to remain powerful, each of us must identify our own Kryptonite and guard against it, because just like Superman long term exposure will kill us and our effectiveness.

Lesson Number Five

Guard against your vulnerabilities.

"On King! On you huskies!"

Recognize that line? That is what Sergeant Preston of the Yukon said every time he jumped on his dog sled and started off on another exciting adventure. And I believe that part of what every good leader must understand is contained therein.

Sergeant Preston understood that he must rely on others to move forward. He used his dogs. He took care of them and treated them first class in every way. He recognized among them a leader, his faithful lead dog, King. He put King out in front because King understood his words, his direction, his mission. They formed a bond based on trust and good communication.

All of us must understand that it is impossible to move forward alone. We must rely on others. Just like Sergeant Preston we have to look at our employees and spot the natural leadership abilities that some of them possess. Then we must pull them out, form a bond, learn to communicate with them, develop trust, then put them out in front so they can help us lead others.

Lesson Number Six

Pick out the leaders among employees and rely on them to lead others.

Another lesson we can learn from Sergeant Preston is that in directing his dogs toward their destination, he never used a whip. Instead, he encouraged them with his words.

He never yelled, "You stupid dogs, if you would just pull harder we could get there faster!" No, he yelled out words of encouragement to them. "You can do it! I know you can! Good dogs!" We could all do better by remembering to encourage others through our words. In fact, the word "encourage" means "to put courage into." The word "discourage" means "to take courage out of." Our words do just that. They either put the courage into or take the courage out of our employees.

Lesson Number Seven
Use words of encouragement to move employees forward.

On a fiery horse with the speed of light, a cloud of dust and a hearty "Hi Yo Silver!" The Lone Ranger rides again!

My number one hero of all time . . . The Lone Ranger. Those words, that music! I heard the other day that the definition of a true intellectual is a person who can hear the William Tell Overture and not think of The Lone Ranger. I don't even want to know people like that!

So what does a cowboy in a mask on a white horse have to teach us about leadership? Plenty! First, The Lone Ranger never killed anyone. He did shoot a few, but he never shot to kill, only to wound them and slow them down so he could capture them and take them to the

Sheriff so the Law could punish them in its own way. Great lesson there. Sometimes, we think we win by killing out the competition. Wrong. We don't have to kill out the competition. We wound them by being smarter than they are. We wound them by serving our customers better than they do. We wound them by training our employees so they can sell better and serve better. When we do those kinds of things, we wound our competitors and they are brought to justice and the Law punishes them in its own way. Much like the bad guys that The Lone Ranger dealt with, they either get rehabilitated or they go away.

Lesson Number Eight

We hurt our competitors most by helping our employees be better at what they do.

The Lone Ranger did what he did because it was simply the right thing to do. He didn't do it for the money. He never took the reward when it was offered. He didn't attack the bad guys out of a sense of revenge. He never tried to "get back" at others because he had been wronged. He didn't do things just to show off. He didn't have to gloat over the fact that he had the best horse or used silver bullets or had a blue double knit jump suit when every one else in the old West was wearing dirty jeans and ragged shirts. No, The Lone Ranger always did every thing because it was the right thing to do. His motives were pure. He was on the side of right. He embodied the slogan, "To protect and serve."

As leaders, we must be the same way. We have to evaluate our motive and make sure that any action we take is done to protect and to serve. We have to do what we do because it is the right thing to do. We must abandon pride, revenge, and monetary reward. We have to know and trust the fact that we will always have more than enough when our motives are pure and we stand for what is right regardless of the circumstances.

Lesson Number Nine
Our motive must always be based in service to others.

The Lone Ranger had a symbol. It was the silver bullet. He always left one behind wherever he went as a reminder of what he believed in and what he stood for. I know that he was known for lots of things and there were many symbols. For instance, there was Tonto, his faithful companion. I think we all need a faithful companion who will go with us, stand beside us, and watch our backs. A great idea for any leader. Then there was the mask. Important because people never knew who he was. Significant because it is a reminder that it is not important for people to know who we are or that we get all the credit. As leaders we must remember to let the credit go to others. And then there was the great white horse Silver. Another good one, because I think we all need first class transportation. But no one can doubt that the silver bullet was the most significant symbol. Mainly because all the others — Tonto, the mask, the great white horse — left when he did. Only the silver bullet remained as a symbol of what he stood for and believed in.

We all leave symbols behind. They aren't silver bullets. Instead they are our products and service, our smile, our handshake, the letter we write, the phone call we make, the words we use. As leaders we have to understand that every time we come in contact with any one else we leave behind a symbol of what we stand for and believe in. And even though we may be long gone, the symbol stays behind.

Lesson Number Ten.
All that we do creates a symbol of what we believe in and stand for in the minds of others, and will remain there long after we are gone.

Yes, I may have watched too much television when I was a kid. But the lessons I learned from my make-believe heroes have served me well. I hope on your journey to becoming a more effective leader that these lessons serve you well too!

ABOUT THE AUTHOR

LARRY WINGET, CSP

Larry Winget began life on a chicken ranch in Muskogee, Oklahoma. He has driven a bookmobile and was one of the first male telephone operators in the Bell System. He has shoveled manure, swept floors, sold, managed, and been the company president. He has experienced both incredible business success and total business failure. However, he is proof that you can go belly-up in business without going face down in failure.

Larry is currently an internationally recognized speaker and seminar leader. He is the author of more than a dozen books and the creator of many audio/video learning systems, as well as lots of other unique personal development products.

Larry is an active member of the National Speakers Association, a charter member of the Oklahoma Speakers Association, and a Certified Speaking Professional (CSP).

He speaks on the subjects of Success, Leadership, Teambuilding, Being Customer Obsessed, and Prosperity. He is also widely known as a humorist and all 'round funny guy. Regardless of the topic, you can be assured that his material is centered around universal principles that will work for anyone, at any time, and in any business. Plus, Larry reads over one hundred books per year to make sure that his stuff is current and that he knows what he's talking about.

Larry believes that success in either our personal or professional life is not hard. It simply comes down to knowing what to do and doing it. He is committed to helping everyone understand that they deserve the best and can have it, when they follow a few simple principles. Known for his unique style, Larry's down-to-earth, humorous, bottom-line approach makes his "stuff" fresh, fun, and easy to implement.

Larry Winget has discovered his uniqueness and learned to exploit it in the service of others. His symbol is the exclamation point. His heroes are Tarzan, Superman, and The Lone Ranger. His dogs are Elvis and Nixon. His wife is Rose Mary. His boys, Tyler and Patrick. His philosophy is, "Expect the best. Be prepared for the worst. Celebrate it all!"

ORDER FORM

For Fastest Service
Call TOLL-FREE

1-800-749-4597

10:00 am - 3:00 pm, weekdays, CST

24 Hour Fax Line

918-747-3185

1232 E. 25th St, TULSA OK 74114

QUANTITY DISCOUNTS

Are available on all of Larry's STUFF. Call for details.

For Seminar Information Call:

1-800-749-4597

1-918-745-6606

SHIPPING & HANDLING WITHIN USA

If Sub Total amount is:

0 - 25.00	$ 3.00
25.01 - 100.00	$ 6.00
100.01 - 200.00	$10.00
200.01 - 300.00	$12.00

Call for rates on purchases over $300.

SHIPPING & HANDLING TO CANADA

If Sub Total amount is:

0 - 25.00	$ 5.00
25.01 - 100.00	$ 8.00
100.01 - 200.00	$12.00
200.01 - 300.00	$15.00

Call for rates on purchases over $300.

Rates do not include duty, taxes or customs charges that COULD be charged at the border

Larry's Stuff

	Unit Cost	Quantity	Amount
Books			
The Simple Way To Success	$12.95		
Money Stuff	$11.95		
Stuff That Works Every Single Day	$ 9.95		
The Little Red Book Of Stuff That Works	$ 7.95		
Just Do This Stuff	$ 7.95		
101 Things That Make You Say UNGAWA!	$ 5.95		
Only The Best On Success	$11.95		
Only The Best On Customer Service	$11.95		
Only The Best On Leadership	$11.95		
Profound Stuff	$ 9.95		
Larry's Library (all TEN above)	$80.00		
Audio			
Larry – LIVE!	$ 9.95		
Video			
Simple Way To Success	$39.95		
We're All In This Together	$39.95		
Learning Systems			
How To Get Booked And Make Money- FAST!...(4 audios)	$39.95		
Other Stuff			
How To Write A Book ...*Book*	$ 11.95		
Exclamation Point (!) *pin*	$ 5.00		
UNGAWA! *coffee mug*	$ 8.95		
Shut Up, Stop Whining And Get A Life *coffee mug*	$ 8.95		
Winning Words Mini-Posters	$17.95		
Stuff That Works Every Single Day (50)	$ 9.95		
The Three Reasons We Are Here (50)	$ 9.95		
Pat On The Back (50)	$ 9.95		
Ten Commandments For Being Customer Focused (50)	$ 9.95		
This Day (50)	$ 9.95		
Money Stuff Affirmation Cards (50)	$ 9.95		
Thanks Cards (100)	$ 9.95		
Expect The Best Poster, Framed	$12.95		
UNGAWA GEAR			
UNGAWA! *T-shirt (XL or XXL)*	$17.95		
No Doubts Allowed *T-shirt (XL or XXL)*	$17.95		
Customers Are Everything *T-shirt (XL or XXL)*	$17.95		
Shut Up, Stop Whining And Get A Life *T-shirt (XL or XXL)*	$17.95		
Larry – World Tour *T-shirt (XL or XXL)*	$17.95		
Shut Up, Stop Whining And Get A Life *hat*	$16.95		

Sub Total ______

Please use chart at left for figuring **Shipping & Handling** ______

TOTAL ______

Name ______ Date ______

Company ______

STREET Address ______

City/Province ______

Zip/Postal Code ______ Country ______ Day Phone ______

Method of Payment: ☐ VISA ☐ Mastercard ☐ Check/Money Order Enclosed

Card No. ______

Exp. date ______ Signature ______

2

Only The BEST

V^3 ... The Power Of Synergistic Leadership

By

Sam Silverstein

V^3 … The Power Of Synergistic Leadership

Sam Silverstein

Values, veneration and vision are the three elements of quality leadership. Used individually, your organization can expect to see a minor impact. Used together, these concepts create a powerful synergistic force that can turn failing organizational environments into profitable and marketable companies. This synergistic force is the difference between the organization that will be going out of business and the one that will dominate and lead the industry into the next millennium. The key to any successful organization is a leader who can inspire the team to greater heights. Using values, veneration and vision, you can create a synergy within your company that will enable your employees to achieve higher levels of productivity, better morale, improved customer service and increased profits.

Synergy is an elusive force. It's like the wind. You

can't see it and you can't touch it, but you know it's happening. Accessing synergy is like trying to access the wind. Sometimes you think you have nothing to do with creating synergy, but you do have something to do with it. Hitler and Gandhi were both powerful synergistic leaders. Hitler chose to use his leadership power in negative and destructive ways, while Gandhi chose a propitious and positive application. You see, the system works no matter where you are coming from when you work it.

To effectively implement synergistic leadership, a strong foundation must be laid. This foundation is based on understanding and mastering the concept of ***change***.

Change is the essence of progress. Without a commitment to change, you cannot have any meaningful improvement in your life or organization. A great many people appear to resist change, but they're really just disheartened by previously unfulfilled promises of change. What seems to be resistance is really fear of another disappointment. Improvement comes through altering, modifying and transforming. Old thinking will not yield new solutions. If you have limited thinking, you will have limited plans. Change involves an expansion in thinking. A commitment to change means opening your mind, realizing the need to make improvements in your habits and behaviors and being able to consider new concepts so you can have the creative plans necessary to achieve your vision. By opening up to change, all members of your team will be able to create the new solutions necessary to transform your organization into a market leader.

VALUES

Values are the cornerstone of all individuals and of any organization. It is critical that you first look to define and understand your own values, then look to define the organizational values. What is it that you really stand for? What are you willing to do to get new business? What are you not willing to do to get that new account? These questions must be answered before personal and organizational leadership can progress.

Quality organizations don't change their values over time. They look for ways to change the application of a time proven set of core values. As industries evolve, product lines change, markets may change, customers may change, but a consistent core organizational value system will be your foundation of strength and long term success. Your values are the rules by which you play the game. It's much easier to make a decision when you have a well defined value system on which to base your decisions.

Define your personal values and your organizations values. Dig deep inside and seek out what means the most. You will find a basis for strength and a foundation for implementation of synergistic leadership.

Most people know what they don't want and not what they do want. To better understand what it is that qualifies as our core values, let's consider the following situation. My driveway is 100 feet long. You are at one end of my driveway and I am standing at the other end. I have a $100.00 bill in my hand and offer it to you if you will walk down my driveway and get it. Will you? Most people would. Now, consider the following. I have covered my driveway with a bed of hot coals. The coals cover the driveway from end to end and side to side. Will you walk through the fire hot coals for the $100.00? My guess is no. Now, I'm going to take your shoes and socks away so you are completely barefoot. There is a fence lining each side of my driveway. The fire hot coals are 12 inches deep. I am holding a bag with one-hundred-thousand-dollars in it. Will you walk down my driveway for the money? My guess is still no. I have placed a dozen 5-gallon cans of gasoline along the driveway. Taped to the sides of the cans are several sticks of dynamite. There is a fan blowing on the coals and they are really heating up. There will be an explosion at any moment. To sweeten the deal, I am holding a briefcase with one million dollars in it. Would you walk through the fire hot coals? My guess is that the answer is still no. Let's make one last change to this scenario. I am holding your daughter (son, mother, father) over one of the cans of gasoline. Now, will you walk down the driveway?

The bottom line is: What are you willing to "walk

through fire" for? The answer to this question is the basis for your core values.

VENERATION

Andrew Carnegie once said, "You must capture and keep the heart of the original and supremely able man before his brain can do its best." By first understanding what is at the core of the team members around you, you will be able to serve them and allow them to reach their fullest potential. You should not only recognize that there are differences among your team members, but also value those differences.

In many organizations, employees (your internal customers) don't feel like they are part of a team. They don't feel valued. They feel as if no one understands their goals, desires or ambitions.

The Council of Communication Management surveyed 705 employees in 70 companies of all sizes and industries. Here is what they found:

- Sixty-four percent don't believe what management says.
- Sixty-one percent feel management doesn't inform them well about company plans.
- Fifty-four percent feel management doesn't explain decisions very well.

Understanding each individual team member's needs and values will enable you to serve them and create an atmosphere of trust and common cause. It's really very simple … if you help your employees achieve their goals, they will help you achieve yours. Team members help other team members. It's an unwritten universal law. Serve your team. They will feel the team spirit and help everyone on that team achieve higher levels of performance.

Companies have two types of customers, internal and external. Your team members are your internal customers and they should be treated as your external customers deserve to be treated. Basically, treat your internal customers not as you would want to be treated, but as ***they*** would want to be treated. This is the highest level of customer service. If you are able to deliver that level of service to your internal customers, you'll be amazed at the loyalty you create.

Veneration also means shaping the right work atmosphere. It is critical that we create a work environment that promotes creative thinking, an openness to change and rewards good effort. All fear must be driven from the workplace. Team members must feel as if they can try new ideas without the risk of persecution if they don't achieve success. Only then will you unleash the power of all individuals and create an atmosphere that promotes growth.

VISION

Just as individuals need goals and a personal vision, every organization needs a vision. This is a unified picture of what everyone on the team is striving to achieve. The clearer the concept, the more likely your team will achieve their goal.

There are three elements inherent in a good vision. To create your company's own vision, have your entire team answer the following questions. Then, begin boiling the answers down until you create your own organizational vision.

What do you do?
How do you do it?
For whom do you do it?

Our company vision is:

Through speaking, recording, and writing we give people the information and tools necessary to define, reach for and achieve their personal and professional goals.

If you use these guidelines, you will be able to create a meaningful vision statement that will serve as the guiding light for your organization. The vision statement must come from the entire team. This is not a top down exercise, but rather a group project that should involve as many people in your organization as possible. If the vision is created by the group, then the group will do whatever it takes to realize that vision.

Knowing what you stand for and what you desire to achieve will allow you to define your vision so vividly you will be able to draw on the energy created by that vision of the future to do what is necessary today to achieve it.

While on a fishing trip to Canada with my son Geoffrey, an interesting thing happened. Geoff and I were on our way forty miles down river to a base cabin to spend the night. On the way down, our guide pointed out a nest in the top of a tree and standing proud over the nest was a beautiful bald eagle. What a sight!

Upon arriving at the cabin, I mentioned the eagle to others in our group. One fellow stated that he saw forty-seven eagles on the way down the river. He was looking for eagles and found them. We were watching the shore and looking for animals visiting the stream for water.

More often than not, if you are looking for something, you will find it. If you are looking up, you'll see eagles. If you are looking for something else, you will see that. Know what it is you desire. Look for it. Work for it. In the end, you will achieve your goals.

Values, veneration and vision do not achieve results. You do. It is your responsibility to take these concepts and apply them to your organization. The only way to do that is to open yourself and your organization to change. With the onset of the new millennium, change is inevitable. Why wait? If you think it sounds good on paper, imagine what it's like when you see it in action.

Several years ago, my manufacturing firm, Delsan Industries, went from years of growth and profits to stagnation and red ink. Customers wanted their orders made in two to three weeks and it took us six to eight. Our quality was inconsistent and morale in the plant was at an all time low. We realized that major changes needed to be made in order to survive. Times had changed and management had to change their philosophy on how the business was run. We talked to the people on the line and shared our challenges with them. We discussed what we needed to achieve in order to not just survive, but thrive. The workers expressed that they wanted to be involved in the production layout, decisions on who would work on their production teams and how incoming manufacturing orders were scheduled. We spent many hours, working together as teams, addressing all the issues at hand. All company groups had the opportunity to have input, to say what their needs were in order to achieve the company wide vision. Many months of planning and then implementation went into restructuring the company. As a result, production time dropped to five working days and customers loved the consistent quality. One account even said they would have to rent extra storage space to handle the regular flow of finished products. The best news was that red ink returned to black.

Our positive results were possible because we knew what we stood for as a company and we learned what was important to everyone else on the team. Together we created our vision of the future and then achieved it.

The difference between management and leadership is this: Management administers past ideas, implements existing systems and maintains existing relationships. Leadership creates the future, with and through people.

So, the question I ask you now is: Do you want to manage and be in charge of the past or do you want to lead and create the future?

About The Author

Sam Silverstein

Entrepreneur Sam Silverstein has a solid track record of building million dollar dreams. The numbers speak for themselves—in one business alone he sold over 100 million dollars of products and services. He successfully sold that business to a Fortune 500 company. Using his proven system for success and his ideas on leadership, Sam has helped companies nationwide become more effective in dealing with leadership, performance and solution based selling techniques. He has shared his secrets for success in his newest book, *The Success Model,* and shows audiences that success has always been within their grasp if they only accept responsibility for it.

To bring his message directly to his audiences, Sam creates a computer driven multimedia extravaganza customized for each group. He utilizes pictures of people in attendance in addition to selections from his inventory of over 20,000 photographs. Sam transforms keynote sessions into a memory attendees will never forget with his big picture ideas and content driven message.

Through the use of humorous anecdotes and moving stories, Sam paints a vibrant picture of what it takes to be a successful leader. Then, with simple step-by-step instruction, he takes his audience through the process so they can implement the skills and techniques into their personal and professional lives.

Sam earned his Bachelor of Business Administration at the University of Georgia and his Masters in Business Administration from Washington University in St. Louis. He is a past president of the Gateway Chapter of the National Speakers Association. Sam is an avid marathoner. He and his wife, Renee, have four children and live in a suburb of St. Louis.

His winning program will make you a better leader, a better communicator, and most of all, show you how ***You Are The Star***.

Sam's most frequently requested programs:

V3...The Power Of Synergistic Leadership

Solution Based Selling In Competitive Markets

The Success Model

You Are The Star

Mastering Change For Competitive Advantage

Other Products

The Success Model™ $19.95
In this 242 page hardback book, you will learn the five step system for personal and professional achievement. Fifty-seven key words that exemplify the success philosophy are explained with step by step instructions for easy implementation. Quick reading and to-the-point chapters give you the information you need to achieve your goals and enhance your life.

The Success Model $29.95
A three tape audio cassette learning system detailing The Success Model system for personal and professional achievement. Learn how to organize your business and personal life for success, overcome the fears that are holding you back, and gain balance in all seven major areas of life. The information contained on these tapes will help you understand not only what to do, but guide you through with step-by-step instruction.

The Success Model $149.95
This fast paced video learning system contains over two and one-half hours of step by step instruction on how to use The Success Model for professional and personal achievement. Learn how to determine what you want and how to attain it. A complete workbook to track your success is included.

Please include $5.00 shipping and handling
Mastercard and Visa welcome

For additional information on Sam Silverstein's custom audio and video learning systems and keynote presentations and seminars, please contact:

Sam Silverstein Enterprises, Inc.
121 Bellington Ln. Suite #400
St. Louis, MO 63141-6118
314-878-9252 888-MOTIVATE (668-4828)
FAX 314-878-1970

3

Only The **BEST**

"...when in command, COMMAND!"

By

Keith D. Harrell

and

Ralph Bianco

"...when in command, COMMAND!"

KEITH D. HARRELL & RALPH BIANCO

Military generals and admirals have always said, *"...when in command, Command!"*. My sister, a police captain, illustrated the point well. Her story went something like this: police radio advised her of a shots fired call with a possible barricaded man. As she arrived to the location she could see several of her officers, who had taken cover behind their patrol vehicles, in front of the subject's home. The barricaded subject was constantly firing his weapon from his front porch then retreating back inside of his house. She stated, "could you imagine me asking police radio to contact my TQM [Total Quality Management] team so that we could brainstorm a solution to this current problem? I don't think so!" The citizens of that city had an expectation of her, as the leader of that patrol shift, to resolve that problem. Her officers, who were in the line of fire, had an expectation that she would resolve the problem, and her superiors expected her to resolve the problem. It was obvious to her, as the leader in that organization, that the expectation was clear: *"...when in command, Command!"*

A leader, when in command, will analyze the organizational environment, develop a plan and strategy and provide leadership to achieve successful results. A leader, when in command, recognizes that only through individual example can the group even hope to realize such results. Understanding and implementing this principle is a blueprint for organizational success that can distinguish *you* from other leaders and consequently *your* group from all others. How can you demonstrate a commanding leadership so that each sphere of influence within your life can achieve extraordinary results and success as a result of your personal leadership? The first step is to recognize the environment.

We live in an environment of perpetual change which requires perpetual leadership. A stationary automobile requires no leadership and accomplishes nothing. While in motion, however, the driver provides the necessary leadership to guide the vehicle's occupants to a safe and timely destination while fulfilling the mission of providing transportation. Similarly, a static organization requires no leadership and provides no growth and therefore no opportunity. Today's leader clearly understands this dilemma and recognizes that the successful organization must embrace change and foster growth and that the leader is indeed, an agent, manager, and instigator of change.

I recently had the opportunity to consult with a close friend of mine, who was vice president in charge of marketing, with a small software development company that was languishing. The fact that their annual sales and profits deteriorated for three successive years was no surprise to me. Their management, business plan, sales and customer service teams had remained intact and unchanged during this same period. Nevertheless, the company president was perplexed because four years prior, the company was highly successful and was named to Inc. magazine's fastest growing company list. What had occurred was the company president failed to recognize the leadership environment. Having been successful was no guarantee of future success. In fact, success became symptomatic of the disease: status-quo. Since the products, services, pricing, etc., offered four years ago made the company successful, the company leadership believed that change was therefore not warranted.

The leadership environment is fraught with uncertainty, limited resources, changing priorities, and perpetual distraction. Successful leaders anticipate these obstacles through the planning process, maintain flexibility and always stay focused. Successful leaders also know that there are only two constants in the leadership environment: people and change, and that these two dynamics are inextricably linked.

Change can only occur when people embrace it; people will only embrace change when they clearly understand the opportunity associated with it. Moreover, astute leaders recognize the leadership environment and realize that their mission transcends it.

No matter what the nature of the organization, team success is invariably the result of the collective effort of diverse individuals working in harmony to achieve a common goal. It is the result of the combined forces of a shared vision, focused commitment and "can do, will do" attitude. It is the result of a leadership process that assembles, develops, and allocates human resources necessary in producing required results. It is the result of a leader who clearly plans, directs, communicates and implements a strategy that every follower believes is the path to personal and collective success. It is the result of a *positive winning attitude* that makes us believe not only in our common goal and each other, but ourselves.

"We have been technically excellent but process poor, and we have to change" said Boeing Chief Executive Frank Schrontz prior to the launch of the 777 aircraft. At the time, Boeing sales had dropped more than 25% in two years, European Airbus Industrie was providing stiff competition and Boeing was trimming its work force by 50,000 to cut expenses and maintain profitability. Schrontz recognized that dramatic and pervasive change was necessary for the organization to survive and grow.

In it's roll-out advertising campaign, the Boeing company attributed the realization of the 777 commercial jetliner to each member of the Boeing team. Undoubtedly, the collective efforts of designers, riveters, schedulers, accountants, et al., all contributed to what is arguably, the finest commercial aircraft in operation in the world today. Yet, without the leadership of Frank Schrontz it is highly unlikely that the Boeing 777 would be flying and setting the standard for commercial aviation today. Quite simply, organizational success was achieved through the demonstrated *leadership* of a *leader* in a position of *leadership.*

Leadership is defined as the ability or capacity to lead. Attitude is defined as a feeling or state of mind. Extraordinarily successful leaders have the ability to inspire ordinary people to accomplish extraordinary goals. Successful leaders are personally committed to a goal, are passionate about achieving it, and inspire others to follow.

The essence of leadership and the characteristics of a leader are well documented. President Dwight Eisenhower summarized leadership as "The art of getting someone else to do something that you want done because he wants to do it". Although there are more elaborate definitions, this captures the fundamental ingredient of a leader managing in a dynamic environment focused on successful results. Perhaps more meaningful, and every bit as significant, are the everyday examples of leadership we have witnessed through the actions of parents, coaches, mentors and friends.

I was always amazed at how my dad got me to accomplish tasks I never had the desire to complete. What I didn't realize at the time was that my father would use my desire to succeed in one field, such as basketball, to help me see the need to continue my education, the goal he had set for both myself and my sister. My goal was to be an NBA star. My father would persuade me at each step that getting good grades would help me reach my goal. If I got good grades in high school, I would be recruited by the best colleges to play basketball. And of course, if I did well in college and maintained my academic eligibility for four years, I would be seen by the best scouts and drafted high in the NBA. Well, I did not get drafted by the NBA but I did receive a Bachelor of Arts Degree.

My father recognized his leadership role within our family and he definitely adhered to the philosophy of *"...when in command, Command!"* Every successful team, organization, company, family or individual possesses a goal and a standard-bearer of that goal. Whether it's winning a championship, being the most profitable, garnishing the greatest industry market share or achieving spiritual enrichment, each environment requires leadership to inspire and reinforce the accomplishment of its mission or goal.

How can you demonstrate the leadership qualities to make not only your professional lives successful, but also your community, church and family?

[1] **Analyze the organizational environment:**

- Search for opportunities
- Examine and question the status quo
- Experiment and take risk
- Be an agent for change
- Accept challenges; give challenges
- Understand the teams strengths and weaknesses

[2] **Develop a plan and strategy:**

- Envision the future
- Enlist others, know your people
- Foster collaboration
- Strengthen others, make others the owner of the dream
- Emphasize long-term and mutual benefits
- Articulate the shared goals and vision
- Clearly plan, direct and communicate strategies

[3] **Provide leadership to achieve extraordinary results:**

- Model the way
- Trust subordinates and delegate authority
- Plan small wins
- Recognize individual contributions
- Celebrate accomplishments

[4] **Command, when in command!**

- Be confident in your ability to lead
- Attitude is everything

Not every individual has the desire to be a corporate leader, but each of us should strive to be the best leader of our individual destinies. Extraordinary success should be each of our goals and extraordinary success requires extraordinary confidence. Olympic athletes train and work harder than ordinary athletes and therefore possess the confidence to compete for and become the world's best. So it is with extraordinary leaders. These individuals "train" to know and understand the team's strengths and weaknesses; articulate the shared goal and vision; trust subordinates and delegate authority to them; and invite dissent and encourage risk. By engaging in this process the leader gains the confidence that, in turn, inspires confidence. When people are inspired they rise to new heights and regard problems as challenges and challenges as opportunities. When this occurs, a *"...when in command, Command!"* leader has emerged to take ordinary teams, organizations, groups or families to extraordinary success.

About The Authors

Keith D. Harrell

Keith Harrell is a former IBM marketing executive and was one of their top training instructors with more than 13 years corporate experience. He has traveled around the world impacting the professional and personal lives of his clients. As a speaker, trainer, consultant, and author, Keith is highly recognized for his innovative and enlightening presentations. His high level of energy, enthusiasm, and powerful messages are exhilarating. Keith's unique and charismatic style of delivery compels participants to take a "fix-it" or "kick-it" approach toward desired changes in attitude, increased confidence and productivity. Keith is described by his clients as dynamic, humorous and motivational.

Ralph Bianco

Ralph Bianco is a consultant for Harrell & Associates, Ltd., who specializes in sales, marketing and management development. Ralph has a degree in business administration from the University of Notre Dame and has held various sales, marketing, and general management positions at IBM, The Boeing Company and Pacific Telesis. In addition, he has successfully established and developed national sales organizations for privately held firms and transitioned them into profitable, publicly held corporations. He has assisted many companies, particularly in the high-tech industry, in achieving their business objectives and sustaining controlled profitable growth while providing management training and consulting services.

Other Products

Attitude is Everything: A Tune-up to Enhance Your Life. This best-selling book provides fundamental techniques to guide you towards establishing and maintaining a positive outlook that will enhance your personal and professional life $20.00

Attitude is Everything Audio Tape Series (2 tapes). This tape series includes highlights of Keith's live presentation that both educate and entertain 24.00

Attitude is Everything Audio Tape. Keith's most popular keynote address which includes practical tips on how to maintain a positive life-enhancing attitude. 12.00

Self-Confidence: The Key to Your Success Audio Tape. This exciting tape provides simple and effective techniques to enhance individual self-confidence 12.00

Change: The Power for Growth Audio Tape. Keith discusses change embracing versus change resisting and how to seize the opportunities that change present. 12.00

Attitude is Everything PC Screensaver. A Windows based screensaver that provides over 1,000 affirmations on enhancing your personal and professional life. 20.00

For more information or to order contact:

Harrell Performance Group, Inc.
4234 North Winfield Scott Plaza, Suite 103
Scottsdale, AZ 85251
(800) 451-3190 • (602) 423-5580 • Fax (602) 423-0526

VISA, MasterCard and American Express accepted.
Please add $5.00 for shipping and handling.

Please inquire about new soon to be released audio and video products.

4

Only The BEST

Whips and Chains Don't Work Like They Used to

By

Roxanne Emmerich

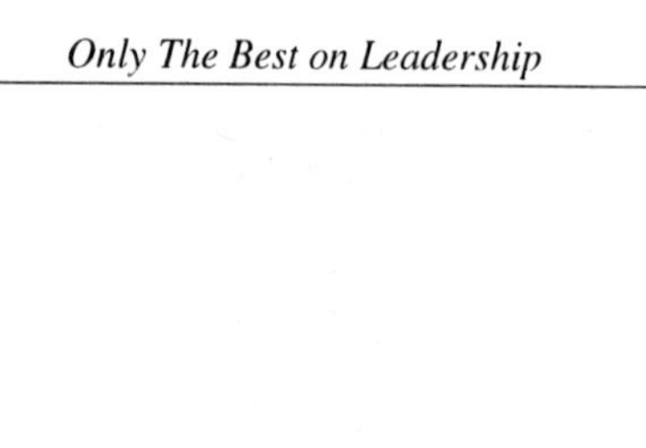

Whips and Chains Don't Work Like They Used to

Roxanne Emmerich

It used to be easy.

To manage people, all you needed to do was chain them to their desks and whip them into a state of fear. They knew that if they didn't meet their quota and make a certain number of calls, they would be replaced by a more compliant servant who would, with eyes glazed over, make numbers.

And then the 90s hit. Employees today are more enlightened. They read books about making a difference, letting their spirits soar, living on purpose, and even how to deal with control freaks. These people want to work on <u>their</u> terms, meet <u>their</u> needs, work <u>their</u> hours, and feel emotionally as well as financially rewarded. They want a life!

Being a leader has moved from a world of pushing to

a world of pulling. Today, leaders must have a vision and enroll others by lighting their hearts, minds, and souls on fire. They need to combine that vision with integrity and an ability to communicate at an emotional level. Leadership is more a learned skill than a natural instinct, and it is a skill that not just the people who have "positions" of leadership must possess. All employees must develop their leadership skills to position themselves to make a difference as a result of their work.

Create a vision.

David Letterman asked Bill Gates, founder of Microsoft, how he got to be the wealthiest man in the world. Without hesitation, Gates replied, "I had a vision— a vision that there could be a computer on every desk in America." Crazy? Maybe so, but that craziness inspired people who found it just intriguing enough to stretch all of their comfort zones to make it happen.

John F. Kennedy had a vision of putting a man on the moon by the end of the decade. At the time of his vision—we know in retrospect—we had only 15 percent of the information needed to accomplish it. It didn't matter. As soon as we heard his vision, our hearts, minds, and souls could see the possibility. Refining the details became a challenge that seemed not only worthy but compelling.

Even small visions create power. I had a vision when

my cleaning lady moved out of state. I didn't need a new cleaning lady. I needed a "wife." I didn't need someone to simply dust, vacuum, and scrub. Because I traveled so much, I needed someone to make my house a home.

Then I met Rosey. She had been cleaning homes for years. When she arrived for her interview, my first thought was that if Santa Claus were a woman, Rosey would be Santa. With bright red checks and a robust, hearty giggle, she immediately presented herself as just the type of person who could make my house a home.

Before I could get my first question out, she informed me, "I don't make beds, wash windows, or do laundry." I looked at her in shock. "Perhaps you don't understand. You see, I don't need a cleaning lady—I need a 'wife'." She wasn't sure how to take that. I quickly clarified by explaining that I needed someone to do the little things to make my house a home. Rosey said in a faint voice, "Oh, I think I can do that."

Her first week Rosey did everything the previous cleaning lady had done, only she did one extra little thing. She put liquid soap in the soap dispenser. I was ecstatic! No one had ever put liquid soap in the soap dispenser. In fact, no one in my house, besides me, had ever put toilet paper on the roll. I sent her a thank-you note and a rose. Every week after that, it kept getting better. She rearranged the furniture—something I never rationalized the need for.

Rosey dusted under the refrigerator. (I didn't even know you could do that.) She bought things to hang on my walls and just left the slips for me to reimburse her. And she even brought gifts for my son.

Of course, as in every relationship, there was conflict. Rosey stopped me one day and announced that she had to tell me something important. (Anyone who has been married for more than a day knows that this is a setup for a fight.) I asked her what was so important. Rosey took a deep breath and sheepishly uttered, "Well, I don't want to hurt your feelings, but . . . I don't like the way you make your beds." I could see she was afraid I would be hurt. I wasn't. I have a philosophy about making beds. Why bother? You just have to redo them every six months anyway. (Well, it's not quite that bad.)

I assured her that my vision meant that she should feel comfortable doing anything necessary to make my house a home. Anything within those boundaries was fair game—no permission needed. As she stripped the bed, she decided to do a few loads of laundry. Every week after that she did all the laundry, and put it all away. Remember, this was the same woman who proclaimed on day one that she didn't make beds, wash dishes or do laundry. She now, by her own inspiration, asked if she could do all three!

One week I called home to tell Rosey I didn't leave

her check out and I would be 30 minutes late because my flight was delayed. She said she'd wait and asked if it would be OK to make the roast in the freezer. I stammered in shock as I replied, "No problem." Not only did she create a culinary delight of roast, au gratin potatoes, vegetables, and dessert, we had enough leftovers for a week. I invited her to join us for dinner. After the first course, she giggled her infamous hearty giggle as she said, "You know, you're all pretty skinny in this house. Would it be all right if I cooked every week? I love to cook." I wanted to shout out in delight, but toned down the excitement in my voice to simply say, "No problem."

Every week, Rosey thought of new and different ways to delight her adopted family. One day stood out as the day she "really got it." It was the day she went out to the garden, cut rhubarb, and made a rhubarb pie! YES! She got the vision!

When she retired, she told me that she never had more fun in all the years she cleaned homes than she had in our house. Funny. I thought I was the one winning. Guess that's how visions work. Everyone wins.

There are three elements of a successful vision:

—It must be short. Most companies have visions like, "To be a leading provider of doorstops in the northwest region by providing outstanding customer service, innovative products, and an above-average rate of return to our blah, blah, blah." This vision, like most, is too long to mean anything and will not be remembered and therefore not lived.

—It should be visual. The human mind can see a picture of a man on the moon or a computer on every desk. It cannot see "innovative" or "customer service oriented." Our actions are not inspired by the concept, but by its visual elements. A good visual statement will imply the non-visual values. For example, "A computer on every desk" implies great service, innovative products, growth orientation and profitability without stating these qualities explicitly.

—It should serve others. When we state that we are in business to make a profit, it is like saying we are alive to breathe. Profits come to leaders who focus on serving their customers and making them successful.

Leaders create a vision that serves others and allows others to meet their needs and get what they want.

Tell the truth at a deeper level.

In the book, The Day America Told the Truth, James Patterson reports that 91 percent of Americans surveyed revealed that they lied regularly. At first glance, that's downright shocking. Upon deeper analysis, it seems probable.

We are socialized to lie. If a boss asks Jack how things are going, he will usually respond with an appropriate, "Fine." The reality may be that Jack wants to say, "Terrible! My office mate needs therapy, I don't have the skills to do my job adequately, and I feel incompetent to do most of my duties. What's more, I think our product is inferior, and your toupee is slipping."

The reality is that if Jack says what is on his mind, he will probably be fired. Jack is smart enough to know that, so he lives with the impostor syndrome, pretending he is adequately placed in the job. Instead of asking for training on the skills he needs, he hopes nobody notices.

At a seminar I put on for a company recently, I had a strong sense that their culture was "nice." They were pleasant to each other, didn't seem to have much conflict, talked at a surface level about their problems, and never really got down to what was holding them back. I stopped the seminar, paused for a painfully long time, and quietly and slowly said, "I think it's time we get the truth out." Some people stopped breathing, while others squirmed while looking for the exit door to see if they could suddenly fake an intestinal virus that would tie them up for hours in the restroom.

I shared with them that it was obvious that they weren't telling the truth. Sure, in private phone conversations they whined about how awful it was. They weren't, however, putting their problems out on the table so they could solve them in a mature way. I had them write down what was really bugging them about working there, then had each of them read what they wrote out loud to a partner. I had them commit to never whine about those problems again by showing them how ridiculous and immature whining was and creating a code they would use with each other whenever they began to do so. I then moved them into a process of solving those problems. They were on fire with excitement about changing the company. The energy in the room was as electric as the transformation of their mindset.

Winners don't whine. They tell the truth and solve the problems. Leaders create a space where it is safe to share the deeper truth without being beheaded. In fact, the most powerful leaders I know are constantly admitting their flaws in public and asking people for help in the areas where they are weak.

Develop emotional literacy.

It always seemed curious to me that some of the most scholarly people I graduated with have been very unsuccessful, while Tim, the guy who barely got by in school, has amassed a fortune. He went into sales. Although he couldn't write a sales letter with appropriate grammar, didn't know how to use his computer to improve his efficiency, and couldn't balance his expense accounts, he seemed to effortlessly and consistently be the highest sales producer out of thousands of sales reps.

What Tim had was emotional intelligence. He knew how to hear what his prospects needed. He knew how to make his customers feel cared for and trusting. He could read from a customer's voice when he or she was having a bad day. He knew when to acknowledge it and call back, and when to acknowledge it and be a friend and confidant for the customer. Tim had the emotional intelligence of a genius.

Leaders develop their emotional intelligence. By constantly asking for feedback and asking people what they really mean when they make a comment, leaders excel in understanding both at an intellectual level and an emotional level.

Being "emotionally literate" means knowing when to give up the need to be right or to jump on the path to problem solving. One who has achieved this can stop and hear emotionally what is really going on. Acknowledging how a person feels is a bonding that rarely happens in most businesses and families. It is, however, one of the most powerful skills we can possess.

Leadership is different than it used to be, yet in many ways it is the same. While the whips and chains of manipulation, control, and managing by fear don't work like they used to, integrity remains paramount.

The future is not what it used to be! The future is a place where people would much rather be pulled into an enticing vision than whipped into doing a "job." The future starts now. Start pulling!

ROXANNE EMMERICH, CSP

Roxanne Emmerich, CSP, is President of The Emmerich Group Inc., a Minneapolis based consulting firm that helps businesses break through to the next level. She is the author of four books including Thank God it's Monday: How to Build a Motivating Workplace and more than 100 articles for various magazines and trade journals.

Successful Meetings magazine has proclaimed Roxanne as one of the top speakers in the country on organizational change. She is the youngest woman business speaker to have received the highest designation of the National Speakers Association, the Certified Speaking Professional, which less than 8% of their membership has attained.

Her reputation for helping organizations improve their productivity earned her an appointment by Governor Tommy Thompson to Wisconsin's highest ranked commission in 28 years. Charged with maximizing the effectiveness of state government, their blueprint for reform is now used as a model for many states and is one of the most widely publicized commission projects ever.

As an executive in charge of starting a new bank and brokerage, she grew deposits form zero to over $35 million in less than two years setting records in growth and profitability. Roxanne co-owned a business that was singled out from over 50,000 others for the top national award in the agri-business industry.

She has coached over one thousand clients including: Northwest Airlines, Dayton Hudson, Monsanto and banks across the country.

For information on speaking or consulting services, contact The Emmerich Group, Inc.

The Emmerich Group, Inc.
One Paramount Plaza
7801 East Bush Lake Road
Suite 360
Minneapolis, MN 55439-3115

1-800-236-5885
e-mail RoxanneEmm@aol.com

OTHER PRODUCTS

Thank God It's Monday: *How to Build a Motivating Workplace*—Book $6.95
Wouldn't it be great to work in a place you couldn't wait to get to? This book gives you sound and immediately applicable ideas for you to use to improve the excitement, fun and productivity in your workplace.

Dancing With Reckless Abandon—Tape $14.95
Roxanne's most popular keynote address—Includes ideas on how to get people thinking about going beyond their job description to viewing their job as seeing what isn't there and making it happen. Learn how to break through your old work patterns of dancing by number to fully thrive using the formula of: Psyche, Systems and Soul.™

That's Not My Job: *How to Make Extraordinary Customer Service Everyone's Focus*—Book $6.95
Thirteen ideas to revolutionize your customer service by changing the focus from satisfaction to customer success.

A Workplace to Die For—Video $39.95
You don't have to kill yourself to create a work environment that is "to die for". This televised interview covers easy ways to make your work environment come alive with more excitement, satisfaction and results.

Only The Best on Customer Service—Book $11.95
The best ideas on customer service from many of the same authors in this book.
If you liked this book—you'll love *Only The Best on Customer Service.*

Want it all? — All 5 items above **.. $60.00**

Please include $5.00 shipping and handling.
Mastercard and Visa are welcome.

For information on all Roxanne's books and learning materials, or to book Roxanne to speak at your next meeting or consult with your group, please contact:

The Emmerich Group, Inc.
One Paramount Plaza
7801 East Bush Lake Rd, Suite 360
Minneapolis, MN 55439-3115
1-800-236-5885
e-mail RoxanneEmm@aol.com

5

Only The BEST

Leadership Charisma: The Light and Laughter at the End of the Tunnel

By

Marc Hardy

Leadership Charisma: The Light and Laughter at the End of the Tunnel

Marc Hardy

John Kennedy had it. Richard Nixon didn't. Ronald Reagan had it. Walter Mondale didn't. Oprah Winfrey has it. Ricki Lake doesn't. Barbara Bush has it; George wishes he knew what it was and how to get it. Charisma. We all know it when we see it, but what is it? An explanation of charisma is elusive, partly because some of its most important elements are hard to define, things so blatant that we look *through* them instead of *at* them. There is no magic formula for charisma; it is the result of a combination of many factors. But if we stand back and survey the common denominators of charismatic leaders, two of these factors become clear:

An unflappable sense of humor and an unshakeable vision of hope.

A sense of humor is a little acknowledged but essential ingredient of charisma. It deflects criticism, makes a bad situation tolerable and puts things in proper perspective. Every charismatic leader has entered a dark tunnel or two and emerged victorious, armed only with the sword of faith in one hand and a shield of laughter in the other. They show those who follow them that there is not only light at the end of every tunnel, but laughter. People are willing to enter the tunnels of life with them because true leaders hold the promise of hope and happiness.

Ralph Waldo Emerson recognized the importance of a sense of humor in his essay *The Comic*, stating that humor "...appears to be an essential element in a fine character. We feel the absence of it as a defect in the noblest and most oracular soul. The perception of the Comic is a tie of sympathy with other men, a pledge of sanity." We are drawn to others who have a sense of humor because we enjoy associating with people who are upbeat versus people who focus on the downside of life. Seeing the lighter side of a situation endears a leader to others by not adding additional weight upon their shoulders. It infers the leader has confidence in life, an air of assurance that all bad things eventually pass or get better.

The ability to laugh at ourselves is probably the most powerful attribute a leader can possess, especially in the political arena. Self deprecating humor has been an asset for charismatic Presidents such as Lincoln, Truman,

Reagan and Clinton. Lincoln and Truman always made fun of themselves, and Reagan and Clinton employed the same strategy to help them get elected.

When Ronald Reagan ran against Walter Mondale in the 1984 Presidential Election, Reagan's advanced age was an issue that was not going to go away. During one of their debates Reagan used wit to defuse his critics, stating that he was not going to make age an issue in his campaign - he was not going to exploit the youth and inexperience of his opponent. The debate crowd and the TV audience went wild with laughter - even Mondale could not keep a straight face. Who won the debate and the presidency is a matter of history.

When then Arkansas Governor Bill Clinton introduced 1988 Democratic Presidential Candidate Michael Dukakis at the Democratic Convention, his twenty minute speech took almost an hour. He became the target of humor on every late night talk show, but Clinton's presidential aspirations took a giant step forward that week. He went on the Tonight Show with Johnny Carson and made fun of himself in front of millions of Americans. In that moment he moved up several notches in the minds of the voting public.

If former President George Bush had taken a few pointers from First Lady Barbara and kept his sense of humor near the end of the 1992 presidential campaign, things might have gone differently. While Bush was pounding away at Clinton's character, Barbara was making humorous comparisons between she and other first ladies. For instance she once made the comment that former First Lady Nancy Reagan was "a size six and so is my leg." Whether you voted for George or not, you couldn't help but like his wife.

Self deprecating humor helps to create a charismatic aura because it gives larger than life personalities a touch of humility - that indeed they are like us and we can trust them. It tells us that they are confident enough to take a few potshots at themselves. Truly great leaders, those who withstand the test of time, know that the bigger the criticism that is levied against them, the more humble they must become. Humility disarms dissenters and most importantly, the media (whom we will deal with in a moment), which could be one reason Reagan and Clinton are considered "Teflon Presidents" - people on which negative images do not stick.

A healthy laugh also helps us think more creatively because it relieves the stress that can block our thought process. It allows us to make associations that are at times absurd so that we start "thinking outside the box." The weight of an absurd problem in a boardroom can be lifted immediately by a well placed witty comment - it can breath life into a seemingly insurmountable challenge. In times of unbearable pressure, people always tend to look to someone with charisma - the person with a healthy sense of levity to break their mental stalemate and free their imaginations from the bars of negativity. As Winston Churchill once stated, "...you cannot deal with the most serious things in the world unless you understand the most amusing."

Even Mother Theresa, who deals with pain and death everyday in the slums of India, encourages humor and laughter in her hospital. Charismatic people know that humor not only helps heal, it also translates into hope. If we can laugh at an obstacle in life, the obstacle begins to lose its power to defeat us. Instead of scaring us it becomes an object of amusement and challenge.

Author of "*The Man Who Would Not Be Defeated*" and fellow speaker W. Mitchell is a prime example of this technique. A paraplegic as a result of an airplane accident, he also suffered severe burns to his body in a motorcycle accident several years ago. His face disfigured by scars, he decided to use humor as a coping mechanism. Already a successful businessman, he decided to run for public office with the slogan, "He's not just another pretty face!" His self deprecating humor made people feel comfortable with his appearance and garnered him the respect of his constituents.

Charismatic business leaders are not motivated by the accumulation of wealth, but the good that wealth can do.

Howard Brembeck, founder of the largest maker of poultry and livestock feeding equipment in the world, has one guiding principle for leading others: a leader must offer hope. When I first read about Howard in a newspaper article he was trying to help save the world. He had developed a concept for nuclear disarmament he titled "The Civilized Defense Plan," a plan that relied on economic power and international law to bring about a world free from the fear of war. Quite an undertaking, even for a successful businessman.

After working with him for several years, it became apparent that Howard is no ordinary businessman. Not a flamboyant leader, he exudes what I call "quiet charisma." A master of self deprecation, he would be the first to decline credit for any of his accomplishments, saying his secret to success is in hiring people that are smarter than himself. But what I observed was that people listen when he speaks because he has a clear, unwavering vision of what is possible - a vision that offers hope, a light at the end of the tunnel.

Part of his secret of success is his "elephant" philosophy - that a leader's vision is often so idealistic and contrary to current reality that it is beyond the belief systems of most people. To the leader the vision is as clear as seeing an elephant in your front yard, but often it is an elephant that others cannot see or even imagine. Only through constantly communicating about your "elephant" will people start to believe it and see it. He believes a leader must paint a picture of a world in which people can see hope and a more positive future for themselves.

When Howard started his business, his vision statement for his company had little to do with money. It offered hope. His goal was to help feed a hungry world, to make poultry so inexpensive to produce that it would be affordable to everyone. A mission of hope like that is a real motivation during times of turmoil and difficulty.

Howard has sold his company and has turned the leadership of his private foundation, the Fourth Freedom Forum, over to a new president. He is now concentrating his efforts on a new vision, the rebuilding of a retreat center dedicated to promoting spiritual growth - a place where people can contemplate a wider perspective of the world and develop a positive outlook and approach to today's challenges. Again a mission of hope and Howard is leading the way, patiently painting pictures of elephants in people's minds until they become reality.

Painting pictures of elephants of hope in a world where the media is seduced by violence and tragedy is not an easy task. The 1996 Olympics in Atlanta, Georgia is a prime example. One would think that the Olympics should be a display of inspiration and hope, but much of the coverage was focused on the bombing in Centennial Park and its aftermath. While it was a tragic event, one could not help but tire at the showing of the same videos over and over of the explosion and people running and screaming. As I watched the redundancy, I became depressed and negative. I asked myself, "What about this information can possibly benefit my life?" The answer; it can't. So I turned off the TV.

The media could be powerfully charismatic, bringing society to new levels of accomplishment, but instead most networks have chosen the low road. The media is in a leadership position, a very influential one, but one which it is always trying to duck. Its spokespeople claim they are entertainment, that they shouldn't be held responsible for people's actions as a result of their programming, and that they don't affect minds - they only reflect life. If the images they portray do not influence the actions of others, then why do advertisers spend billions of dollars on TV every year to influence people? If what the broadcasters claim is true, they would be bankrupt because no one would pay for their programming.

One leader in the media who is paying attention to her influence is Oprah Winfrey. A leader among women, minorities and celebrities, she is using her charisma to bring positive messages to people. She has changed the format of her talk show to reflect hope instead of confusion, unification instead of conflict. She has realized that as people think, they act. If people do not have hope, they live in darkness and make negative decisions. If they live in hope, they gain a sense of self respect and forge their lives in a positive direction.

This is not just pollyannish thinking. Daniel Goleman, author of *Emotional Intelligence*, states, "Hope, modern researchers are finding, does more than offer a bit of solace amid affliction; it plays a surprisingly potent role in life... having hope means that one will not give in to overwhelming anxiety, a defeatist attitude, or depression in the face of difficult challenges or setbacks..." Goleman goes on to cite several studies of students, salespeople and others to support his claim.

But do we really need statistics to tell us that we make better decisions when we are filled with hope and happiness? How many of us have made bad decisions when we were angry or frustrated, decisions we look back on in a better frame of mind and wonder what we were thinking? Possessing hope and humor is not just something that would be nice to have - it is a prerequisite to effective leadership and decision making. They are rare attributes in a society bombarded with negative hopelessness from the radio, TV and in print and people cannot survive and prosper without them.

In a world filled with negative images and sad news every minute of the day, people are starved for positive, charismatic leadership, the kind not motivated by financial gain but that offers a universal cause - one that holds the promise of a better tomorrow, one filled with hope and happiness. There is so much stress and so many nay-sayers in today's world that people will support the teacher, parent, coach, celebrity, clergy, business person and politician who can make them feel positive about themselves and their future. They will walk with the person who locks arms with them and faces adversity with courage. They will follow the leader who shows them the light and laughter at the end of the tunnel.

About The Author

Marc Hardy

As a speaker and author, Marc Hardy's humorous insights on the adversity we encounter in our professional and personal lives have been enjoyed by thousands of people throughout the United States and Canada.

Thought provoking and funny, he redefines the meaning of failure and making mistakes, treating them not as obstacles to success but necessary steps toward success. He draws on his experience in management in profit and not-for-profit organizations for the past 20 years in more than a dozen industries; he has work in construction, factories, jewelry stores, bakeries, and professional theatre.

He served as a reserve police officer and was chosen "Reserve Recruit of the Year", and for seven years was the executive director of a private foundation and think tank.

His degree in Human Resources Management and his diverse background allow him to relate to almost any audience. He has received several awards for outstanding sales and in 1991 was voted one of the top three speakers in the "World Championship of Public Speaking". His articles have appeared in several publications including Bottom Line Business, The American Salesman, Human Resource Professional, Employee Services Management, Business Opportunities Journal, and Mid-America Commerce and Industry, and he is a co-author of Only The Best on Leadership published by WIN Publications.

Programs:

Keynotes:

"Daring Greatly: *How to value adversity, look forward to failure and make our mistakes meaningful"*

"Smooth Stones, Broken Bones And Danger Zones: *Wit and Wisdom from Life's School of Hard Knocks"*

Workshops:

"Creating Leadership Teams: *A Workshop for Not-For-Profit Board Directors, Managers and Employees"*

"Unlimited Influence: *Powerful Presentation Secrets of Professional Speakers and Trainers"*

OTHER PRODUCTS

Audio Tapes:

"Daring Greatly" (One hour Keynote) $10.00

"Unlimited Influence" (Three tape set) $30.00

"Articles On Tape" $10.00

Books:

"Only The Best On Customer Service" $11.95

For information on all Marc's products, or for information regarding speaking engagements, please contact:

Marc Hardy & Associates
58485 Hilly Lane
Elkhart, Indiana 46517-2241
219-295-7600 • 800-850-6509
Fax: 219-522-3355

6

Only The BEST

Leadership in a Time of Change

By

Scott McKain

Leadership in a Time of Change

Scott McKain, CSP, CPAE

One of the questions all of us who study leadership — and those who hope to <u>be</u> leaders in one way or another — are wrestling with is: Does the very nature of leadership change when times are changing?

If you look around you, I am certain you see technology changing. For those of us a bit older, we have seen the progression from typewriters to word processors to mainframes and even desktop and laptop computers. Whole departments have been replaced by a machine. Entire job categories have disappeared. Highly skilled workers, like linotype operators at newspapers, have had to learn the computer or find another trade.

Information is the name of the game and we add new words to our dictionaries ever year — CD-ROM, CDI, satellite conferencing, video phones, the Internet — every day we have new technology to master. No sooner do we learn one machine than it seems that here comes another to replace it.

In addition, we have seen changes in how our professional lives fit into the overall scheme of things.

For example, perhaps you have been involved in a lay-off, or a "R.I.F." (reduction in force). Maybe you've seen it where you work and it may have made you less confident of your future than ever before. Let's face it, it is very difficult to be a leader when you are worried and uncertain about your future.

I remember it was not that long ago that you would join a company as a young person and fully expect to get your watch or pin or ring signifying twenty-five, thirty or forty years with the same organization.

The company was your extended family and they would take care of you, and you would work the rest of your life for that company and retire with a pension. That was just the way it went. It worked that way for your Dad and your Grandfather, why not for you? Today, you see all the lay-offs and changes and plant closings and you wonder if you might be next.

Maybe you are doing very well and you just want to do better, but because of this change, you have less control in your work.

The change is happening <u>to</u> us, not <u>with</u> us.

As a result, many of us find ourselves less in control and less satisfied with what it is we do.

Perhaps all of this change that surrounds us is creating a time that calls for leadership more than ever before.

Change is happening personally too. This has, perhaps, even more of a dramatic impact. We have seen changes around us as everything seems to cost a little bit more, and we seem to have a little bit less at the end of each pay period.

We see the economic pressures that the government is facing in health care, Social Security and foreign trade (to name a few), and we realize that we are the ones who are going to have to pay the bill.

Our personal lives are a little bit faster paced and less fulfilling because we have less quality time together with our families. Many homes now depend on two paychecks and there are enormous pressures that accompany that — especially when there are kids to care for.

We have seen other changes in our personal lives...the videocassette recorder and the microwave oven and cellular phone and on and on. Technological changes are affecting us at work and they are having an impact on us at home, as well.

The result is the same process happens at home that happens at work. We become increasingly pressured and dissatisfied. We never feel we have achieved enough because we are always playing "catch up."

When we're talking about change and the changes that we are going through in our lives, leaders understand that there is good news and bad news.

The bad news is, change is constant. We are always going to have change.

It is bad news because most people do not take advantage of the changes so they can say "yes" to new opportunities. These are the people who are not leaders. They are stuck in a rut, and the cumulative effects of today's changes are going to make it even more difficult for them to deal with innovations in the future.

In other words, the more things change, the tougher it's going to get for people who do not adapt and who refuse to take positive action.

The good news is, change is constant. We are always going to have change.

The good news is that change is going to be constant, because whether you like change or not, you can do what true leaders do: Develop a strategy that can help you and the people you lead stay in control of your lives in these unstable times.

I strongly believe most of us want life to be more than what we currently have. I don't think any one of us is completely satisfied with where we are in life, no matter how much we achieve. For instance, if you were totally satisfied, you wouldn't have bought this book to understand leadership and better your life.

Satisfaction is nothing more than a fancy word for inaction.

Leaders understand that when we are satisfied, we do not grow. When we are contented, we do not change. We just stay put. I want to be happy, but I never want to settle for being merely content. I want fulfillment, but I never want total satisfaction.

Starting over twenty years ago up to this day, I have had the chance to talk with successful leaders all over the world. I have met political leaders including the President of Brazil and three Presidents of the United States. I have talked with movie stars and celebrities and top business people.

Do you know that not one of them expressed total satisfaction with what they had achieved?

I have yet to meet anyone who says: "Well, that's it.

I'm going to quit now. I'm completely satisfied with every aspect of my life."

The main attribute all leaders have in common is that we all want life to be more than it is, no matter how much life currently seems to be. The challenges of the future are so important that when we stop facing the future, we start to die.

It does not matter what age we are, it does not matter how much we have achieved...there is still more out there for the leader.

Let me tell you about the leader I was sitting next to at a banquet when I was 21 years old — Colonel Harlan Sanders of Kentucky Fried Chicken fame.

During dinner, Colonel Sanders asked me if I knew where he had gotten the seed money to develop Kentucky Fried Chicken.

I figured he must have had an investor but he said no, it came from his *first Social Security check.* I have never forgotten that.

It's never too late, it's never too soon. You're never too smart, you're never too dumb. You're never too rich, you're never too poor to take advantage of the changes in your life and become a leader, or enhance your leadership capabilities.

There are many obvious traits and qualities of leadership that we can discuss. However, there are two that are often overlooked that I have seen in leaders I admire.

Humility

Ronald Reagan has become identified by people of all political persuasions as one of the most important leaders of the twentieth century. Former Speaker of the House, Tip O'Neill, often spoke of how he respected Mr. Reagan as a leader, despite their vast political differences. Mr. O'Neill would say that they could disagree without being disagreeable.

In a recent interview to promote a book, political consultant Ed Rollins stated that of all of the thousands of politicians with whom he has worked, Ronald Reagan had the least ego and was the most humble.

Picture how most politicians answer a question from the press. In an often vain effort to sound as they think a leader should sound, most political figures puff themselves up and become very authoritative. While the content of their response might be nothing more than a "definite maybe," the attempt is to sound as if they are in total control of everything.

Now, remember a press conference with President

Reagan. Sam Donaldson would fire a rough question toward the President. Mr. Reagan's eyes would twinkle, his head would tilt, and softly he would begin, "Wel-l-l..."

The approach was irresistible.

As we think about the dramatic changes we are experiencing, the amount and flow of information is perhaps most important. Leaders of the future understand that the old saying, "Knowledge is power" is true. However, they also know that they are no longer able to use the old tactic of hoarding information. They know they cannot lead by keeping their followers ignorant.

Many of the great leaders, such as Harry Truman, have called themselves, "humble servants" of the people they have lead. Yet, in many organizations, leaders have failed to fill this role of leadership. Most leaders picture themselves out in front of the group, pulling them along behind them. Leaders in today's changing times — now more than ever — realize that it is quite possible to lead from the rear, gently steering and pushing the group in the direction that he or she wants to lead.

Humor

An elementary student asked then-Presidential candidate John F. Kennedy, "How did you become a war hero?"

"I had no choice," the future President replied. "They sank my boat."

Leaders of today know that humor is a vital tool in communication. They are not stand-up comedians, but they use merriment to enhance the meaning of what they are saying.

As children we were allowed — encouraged even — to run and laugh and play. As adults, we have our image to protect and if we're having too much fun, we're afraid we won't be perceived as professional. The grimness with which we face life is a tribute to the seriousness with which we view the mess of our human existence. Isn't that ridiculous?

I read a study, conducted at the University of California at Santa Barbara, in which researchers found children laugh ten times more frequently than adults. Children are probably ten times less stressed than adults, too. Don't you think there might be a correlation there? Leaders understand that in stressful times, humor helps us all get along.

It is also important to remember, though, that leadership is stressful. Leaders must have a sense of humor to handle all of the pressures that they will have to face. Was John Kennedy a great leader, in part, because he had a sense of humor? Was he able to handle the challenge of leadership because his sense of humor helped him deal with the enormous stress he had to handle? Of course, the answer for both questions is an unqualified, "Yes!"

Some people who attempt to be leaders try to be more solemn than anyone else. They want people to think that the leader must shoulder all of the burdens and responsibilities of their group. Mark Twain said it: "Martyrdom covers a multitude of sins." Too often leaders assume the martyrs pose so they do not have to stop their own private pity party and get on with the job of leadership.

When you think that humor should not be a part of the vitally important role of a leader, remember this line from a book by Dr. Alan Loy McGinnis. "Pain is inevitable but misery is optional." What a powerful message. "Pain is inevitable but misery is optional." Take the responsibility of leadership very seriously. Don't take yourself too solemnly.

As times change, people change — but <u>values</u> do not have to.

Understand the dynamics of change in these rapidly changing times.

Maintain the important values of humility and humor as the world around you goes crazy.

And, lead with integrity.

Scott McKain

As a professional speaker, seminar leader, and consultant, Scott McKain has received rave reviews over the past 15 years. With topics ranging from customer service and communication, achievement and motivation, Scott can tailor his programs to any audience with a blend of cutting-edge information and sharp humor. He provides solid information in an entertaining package–a winning combination for any audience.

Scott has given presentations for audiences which range in size from 20 to 10,000+, for international companies, state organizations, and non-profits. He has satisfied each one by working with them to customize his presentation to their specific needs, adding a touch of wit to send the message home.

Scott grew up in rural America, and brings his knowledge of "real people" to each presentation he makes. His leadership skills developed early–he was elected a National Officer of FFA, an organization of over half a million members, before graduating from college. Other honors include being on several presidential committees, being named in "Who's Who in the Midwest" and a Jaycees "Outstanding Young Men in America." In addition to his speaking career, Scott also has a successful commentary show syndicated to over 80 stations across the US, Canada, and Australia.

Other Products

Just Say YES! A Step Up To Success! • *The seven cassette, fourteen day program to personal achievement that started it all! As seen on national TV!!! Learn the importance of values and priorities, goal setting and communication, and the "Six Steps Up To Success!" Sold on national television for $79.95 . . . special price for Only The Best readers:* $49.95

Just Say YES! A Step up To Success • *The hot-selling book based on the audio cassette album. With a foreword by baseball hall of famer, Jim Palmer! A must read!!! In bookstores for $29.95 . . . special Only The Best price:* $19.95

Just Say YES! A Step Up To Success! • *A full-hour video of the best of the entertainment and enlightenment of Scott McKain.*
(VHS format only) $19.95

Dragonslayers! • *Scott's first audio program. Recorded live and in-studio. The cassettes of humor and information on change, humor and relationships. (Limited quantities available.)* $19.95

Single audio tape of fun with Scott! *Laugh and learn. some of the best of Scott's classic humor and some new fun with a master of message and merriment!* $10.00

SAVE!!! get the whole package for only $99.95

Visa, Master Card, and American Express accepted.
Please include $4.50 for shipping and handling.

For more information contact:

McKain Performance Group
P. O. Box 24800
Indianapolis, IN 46224
800-297-5844
317-297-5844
FAX 317-297-4621

7

Only The **BEST**

Inspiring Everyday Excellence

By

Lisa Ford

INSPIRING EVERYDAY EXCELLENCE

LISA FORD

Leadership inspires excellence, encouraging others to be their best. And excellence must be renewed and maintained daily. It doesn't just happen on its own. As a leader your challenge is creating an environment where excellence is an everyday habit.

Let's focus on two aspects of excellence, personal and leadership. Personal excellence must be the starting point. Obviously if you don't have personal excellence, you can't lead and inspire it. The five steps to personal excellence are:

1. Love Change

In today's fast paced world you have no choice. You must realize what's worked for you in the past is no guarantee of future success. I hear people saying, "I can't wait until things get back to normal." Well, nothing's going back to normal. The chaos, upheaval and constant change is the norm today.

We resist change for a number of reasons. One is fear

of the unknown. As humans, most of us love control, so the unknown is uncomfortable territory. Two is fear of loss. This could include loss of responsibility, loss of market share, loss of security or loss of a relationship. The third reason is fear of being inadequate. For example, with a new piece of technology, you might ask, "Will I ever learn it, will I look stupid?" It's important to recognize your resistance so you can create strategies to accept change.

When confronted with change, look for the opportunity and lesson. Remember you control your reaction to change. When faced with change, ask "Is there a less destructive way to look at the change?" Don't let yourself start imagining the worst. You can talk yourself into stress or out of it. To keep from imagining the worst, get information about why the change is taking place, how it will affect you and what will be expected of you. The information acts as nourishment to concentrate on the upside of the change.

As a leader your team will look to you for how to react to change. You can either resist or embrace it.

2. Take Risks

If you embrace change quickly, you probably take risks easily. However, there are plenty of people who need to give themselves permission before taking a risk. Here are three questions to ask to get past the discomfort.

What's the worst thing that could happen? Now, most of us ask that and the answer is so frightening we get paralyzed and don't move forward. To get past this inaction, ask the following questions.

-What's likely to happen?
- What's the best that could happen?

The answers will help you focus on the upside of the risk. And by identifying the downside you can minimize the effects by planning your reaction.

And of course, when you take a risk you may not be quite as successful as you had carefully planned. Risk taking and mistake making go hand in hand. Remember the old saying, "A mistake is just another way of doing things." The key is how you handle the mistake. As a leader, your team doesn't necessarily like to see you make a mistake, but they do love to see you admit the mistake. Talk about the failure, the challenge and the lesson. You'll develop lots of risk takers among your team when they realize mistakes and risk taking are accepted and even welcomed. The future belongs to the people who can celebrate failure and move forward.

3. Do Something

People who pursue excellence take action. Do you know those people who constantly talk about what they are going to do and talk and talk and never get around to doing anything? Stop sitting around trading opinions, it's like sitting on the sidelines of a game. You don't get anywhere on the sidelines.

Today's world rewards the people who take action, avoid status quo and get on with doing what they say they're going to do. I heard there was a sign on the Alaskan Highway that reads: "Choose your rut carefully, you'll be in it for the next 200 miles" - not a very pleasant thought.

4. Learn Everyday

Leaders know their skills and knowledge must be state of the art. Your attitude towards learning cascades down to your team. Set goals to be 1% better and smarter tomorrow than you are today. In this marketplace, where layoffs and downsizing are common, you must realize you are your own business. Examine your skills to determine the value you add to your team.

5. Ask for Criticism

Think back to a time you took a golf or tennis lesson, most likely you paid for this lesson! You paid for someone to criticize you, then typically your game worsened before it improved (hopefully). People at work are happy to give you criticism for free! The higher you go in your business, the tougher it is to get honest criticism. Seek feedback and learn how you are perceived. Then tackle areas of weaknesses. This marketplace demands that you add value for your team, organization and customers. To determine your value, get feedback and act on it to improve.

Personal excellence is the starting point for leaders. To inspire excellence in others, let's look at leadership excellence. Here's six steps for effective leaders:

1. Provide a purpose, focus and direction

Teams need to know the "why, where and how" of their role. Does your team know where they are going, how they will get there and why they exist? People need to know what resources and support will be available. Link them with the rest of the organization and tell them what's expected. A compelling purpose will unify a team to move forward and fast.

2. Create Trust

To keep people excited about everyday excellence, you must create trust. To build trust here's a laundry list of ideas. Keep your word. Deliver on your promises. Keep confidences. Make certain behavior and words match. Share credit for successes. Value others input. Treat people as competent and skilled. Be honest. Believe in your people. Remember to behave with courtesy and fairness. Praise people sincerely. Confront problems fast. Follow through on commitments.

Do the opposite of any of these and you will start to destroy the trust among your team. Leaders realize trust is like gasoline in a car. You can not fill the tank once and drive forever. The gas tank must be constantly monitored and refilled. Your team trust is the same. Trust is fragile and fleeting. Keep your eye on the "trust gauge."

3. Listen and Ask Questions

Time and time again, research shows a common trait among leaders is that they listen. Listening is a valuable skill to build and gain respect. Go ask your team, "If you were in my position, what one thing would you change to... (improve the quality of our customer service, create more innovative products, make our team more effective") The best leaders realize they do not have all the answers so they ask lots of questions. Knowing the right questions to ask is a key to leadership.

Remember when you ask for ideas and opinions, you must truly listen, as in shut your mouth. I'm reminded of one of my favorite sayings, "There is a difference between listening and waiting for your turn to talk." Which is your habit?

4. Develop an Attitude That Inspires

The attitude of the leader can be very contagious. Is your attitude one that people want to catch? To inspire everyday excellence, create an attitude of energy and enthusiasm. Do a mental makeover every so often. There is exciting research to indicate the need for a mental makeover. According to Martin Seligman, author of *Learned Optimism*, the best predictor of personal success and everyday excellence is your level of optimism. His work has shown how optimism is essential and how to acquire it. Most of us have a sense of whether we are optimistic or pessimistic. Your goal is to create a habit of optimism. Here's some background on Seligman's research.

Seligman suggested to Metropolitan Life that optimists would be more successful in sales positions. By using his inventory, Met Life hired a group of sales agents who scored high on the optimism scale. And at the same time they hire a group of agents based on traditional hiring methods. The new "optimistic" recruits were dramatically outselling those hired the traditional way. Optimists were outselling the others by 37% in the first two years, which is estimated to boost revenues by $10 million. Seligman explains that the success of optimistic people is in their explanatory style which is how they explain the events that occur in their lives. Optimists see themselves in control of events in their lives. They attribute their success to skill not luck. Optimists view a bad event as a passing, isolated event. Pessimists see the same bad event as something that would naturally happen to them, allow the bad feelings to hover and feel victimized by what happens.

Optimists do not necessarily paint a rosy picture, but they do avoid negative interpretations. Reality is that all people suffer setbacks, how we see the setback makes the difference. A mental makeover to change your attitude to one of optimism may be exactly what you and your team needs. Remember attitude is the first step, then positive action and behavior must follow.

5. Take Leadership Seriously

Your every action is noticed, interpreted and sometimes even discussed. People watch how you spend your time. For example, if you state as the team's purpose "complete dedication to customer service", then people expect you to spend time on customer issues and time with real customers.

A sure fire way to lose the respect of your people is to talk about the team's purpose yet take little action yourself to show the commitment. For example, you may claim your dedication to customers, but spend most of your time on internal issues, financial concerns, little attention to employees who exceed customer's expectations and cost-cutting measures. The old phrase "walk your talk" applies here.

It is absolutely necessary to follow through on what you say. You know that! Take time to check if your behavior is consistent with your words.

6. Have Fun

If you're not having fun, why do it? People want to work in an environment that has spirit and energy. Leaders set the tone for creativity and fun. Today's work force expects a lot more than a paycheck from the workplace. And you certainly know employees are quick to leave for the promise of a more rewarding workplace. There are many leaders who would say when people are having fun, they are more productive, turn out higher quality, and more innovative. Fun pays off on the bottom line.

People look to leaders for so much - direction, expectations and inspiration. Inspiring everyday excellence is important work. Your challenge is maintaining the momentum and focus. Leadership is a learned skill for those who choose that path. Excellence is an attitude. With the leadership skill and excellence attitude, inspiring excellence will become an everyday reality.

Lisa Ford

Author Of The
#1 Selling Business
Videotape Series
"How To Give
Exceptional
Customer Service"

Lisa Ford delivers what her audiences want - practical ideas combined with plenty of opportunities to laugh and relate to her examples. Her content inspires people to increase their personal, team and organization's results.

Lisa is the author of *How To Give Exceptional Customer Service*, the #1selling business videotape series for the last 3 years in the U.S. She has also authored, *Developing A Customer Retention Program*, co-authored *Building A Customer Driven Organization: The Manager's Role* video and audio tapes, and *Personal Power* audiotapes. She specializes in the field of customer service, customer retention, managing, hiring and training for service excellence. Other popular topics offered by Lisa are on leadership, management, everyday excellence and communications.

Lisa's experience includes working with many of the nation's best: SmithKline Beecham, Equitable, Viacom, CSX and Georgia Power. She presents over 100 speeches and seminars yearly across the United States, United Kingdom and Australia.

Over the years, Lisa has customized numerous videos for clients to use in their ongoing training efforts. She is highly rated and a favorite speaker at the International Customer Service Association where she speaks annually.

Audiences love Lisa's energy, enthusiasm, humor, practical techniques and common sense messages. After her presentations, organizations love the change in attitudes, increased awareness and improved results.

Lisa's Programs Include

- ***Why Customer Service Is Not Enough***
  Focus On Satisfaction, Loyalty and Retention
  Exceed Expectations As A Daily Discipline
- ***Everyday Excellence***
  Create And Add Value To Increase Your Results
  Maintain An Attitude Of Enthusiasm
- ***How To Lead And Manage In Today's Crazy Workplace***
  Understand The Role Of The New Manager
  Love And Master Change

OTHER PRODUCTS

How To Give Exceptional Customer Service $299.95
The Nation's best selling video series. 4 volumes plus workbook covering how to make each contact memorable and keep customers satisfied. Great for training sessions.

How To Give Exceptional Customer Service $79.95
4 audio tape program, great for anyone who has contact with customers. Terrific how-to's, stories and examples.

Developing a Customer Retention Program $59.95
4 audio tapes on how to increase repeat business and build loyalty. Lots of action ideas.

Inspiring Everyday Excellence $10.00
An audio tape recorded live, covering personal excellence, service excellence and leadership excellence. Very motivational.

Six Ways To Be A Service Leader $10.00
An audio tape recorded live, with action steps to exceed customer's expectations and lead to inspire great service. Includes Lisa's memorable dry cleaners story.

Please add $4.00 Shipping & Handling

For more information contact:

Ford Group, Inc.
140 Seville Chase
Atlanta, Georgia 30328
770-394-4860 • FAX 770-394-0034

8

Only The BEST

Legacy of Leadership

By

Vic Osteen

LEGACY OF LEADERSHIP

VIC OSTEEN

"An organization without a leader is just a bunch of people with a common zip code."
Robert Townsend

Leadership is the buzzword for personal and business success in today's society. It is discussed and preached at every turn in modern business writings. Leadership has become a hot topic because of its elusive manner. The term "Leadership" or "Leader" evokes a different picture in the mind of each person. Take a moment to think about who comes to mind when you hear the word leader. Is it a political figure, a military commander, a teacher or coach, a parent or friend?

We no longer have the single image of who the leaders are or what constitutes good leadership. Modern society has blurred our image of leadership and the characteristics leaders possess. There can be a very effective leader in one position or situation who possesses a very different set of characteristics or style from another leader in a different situation.

There are however some general characteristics that seem to guide most leaders. Everyone should seek to develop these traits so they may better lead their own life and strive to help those they come in contact with, be it at work, within your family, your church, your social activities or your everyday responsibilities.

"Nurture your mind with great thoughts;
to believe in leadership makes leaders."
Vic Osteen

Leadership is an attitude that is developed by knowing where you are going and being willing to share it with others. To achieve this you must develop yourself and be able to communicate with others. You must know where you are, where you would like to be and have an idea of how to get there. If not, you will be like the conversation in Alice In Wonderland, where Alice asked the Cheshire cat, "would you tell me which way to go from here?" The cat replies, "That depends a good deal on where you want to get to".

Define Your Purpose

"Management asks, "Am I doing things right?"
Leadership asks, "Am I doing the right things?"
Stephen R. Covey

Leaders have asked the question, Why am I here?,

What is it that I want to attain?, What is my intention?, What do I want to bring about? They are big questions to be answered but to truly lead, the answers must be formulated. What is your legacy, what is it that you want to be remembered for, what does your company want to be known as? No matter what external forces act upon you or your business, positive or negative, your purpose should be your guiding light. Without a defined purpose, we vacillate between what seems to be a good idea for the moment and what is best logn term.

Carlyle states that, *"A man without a purpose is like a ship without a rudder."*

For your sake and the sake of those you touch, take the time to define your purpose and the purpose of your organization. Take hold of the rudder you have established, set the course and begin the journey.

"The secret of success is singleness of purpose."
Disraeli

Have Vision

"Where there is no vision the people perish"
Ralph Waldo Emerson

Vision is being able to see the future. What we visualize becomes reality. To move ahead you must look to tomorrow and have a clearly defined picture of what it is that you want for yourself and others. One of the greatest leaders in modern times was President John F. Kennedy. He created a clear vision for this country, landing a man on the moon by the end of the decade. It was one of this country's greatest times of industrial growth and brought a nation together for a common cause. This vision in turn spurred the economy and brought us thousands of new jobs, products, and conveniences.

A leader is an artist with the canvas of tomorrow, for that is all we have and all that we can control. The lines are not drawn, the colors not applied, until the vision is clear.

We need to have dreams, visions, goals of where we want to be for them to become a reality. Think big and we get big; think small and we get small; don't think at all and we get disappointment.

Determine what you want to accomplish and don't be afraid to share it with others. We need to be constantly working toward building a better tomorrow, learning from our past, living today but thinking how it will serve us tomorrow. Today is tough to get through at times, but we do it so we will experience the joys of tomorrow.

We must develop a clear picture for those around us so that they can apply their efforts so we may all succeed.

It is better to look where you're going
than to see where you've been.

Unkown

Communicate

A wise man reflects before he speaks;
a fool speaks and then reflects on
what he has uttered."

Abbe Delille

One of the greatest tools we have is that of communication. Leaders must be people who can get the vision across for it to be captured by others, by those we are attempting to lead. We all communicate, but what is being heard and seen many times is not the message we desire. To be a good communicator, you do not have to be an excellent orator. You do need to be clear and consistent in your message. Nothing screws up people more than saying one thing and acting out another. As we have often heard, "Your actions speak so loudly that I can't hear what you are saying."

Communication takes many forms and skills. Good communicators are good listeners. They hear and attempt to truly understand what is being said to them. Not only the words, but the underlying meaning. Leaders take 100% responsibility to be sure that the message being sent is understood. They see what is going on, knowing that what you see is usually what you get, no matter what you are told. They try to speak the language of the people they are working with to make it easy to understand. They know they are there to serve, not to impress.

Praise

"When the best leaders work is done the people say, "We did it ourselves!"

Lao-tzu

Leaders are willing to give people credit for their effort and reward them for the things they do accomplish. A kind word will motivate a work force more than an envelope stuffed with money. A leader communicates in many forms. Not only the spoken word, but in writing. A note from someone means so much and costs so little. "The palest ink is greater than the strongest memory."

I know a manager at American Airlines who has purchased a set of motivational thank you cards from a catalogue and sends them out when people do a good job on a project or in a meeting. From taking time to do this little thing, to show a little appreciation, she has the most loyal employees, and they in turn think she is the best manager they have ever had.

It is said that, "A Good leader inspires men to have confidence in him; Great leaders inspire men to have confidence in themselves." Encouraging others and serving their emotional needs is true leadership. The only two things people really want are respect and appreciation.

Take Action

"It's the price of leadership to do the thing you believe has to be done at the time it must be done."
Lyndon B. Johnson

It is wonderful and good to have great visions and plans, but a leader must take action for anything to get accomplished. He must mobilize the troops and call for personal responsibility to be successful. A quarterback has to not only call the plays but get the ball and run with it to get the team moving and ultimately score. Mary Kay Ash is at the office early every morning to get her cosmetic empire moving. Jimmy Johnson can be seen running pass patterns with his Super Bowl winning teams. You cannot expect that great ideas or great paychecks are going to create the results that are necessary to win.

"Leadership is more visual than verbal."
Vic Osteen

Be persistent

"Great works are performed, not by strength, but by perseverance. He that shall walk with vigor,

three hours a day will, in seven years, cover a space equal to the circumference of the globe."

Samuel Johnson

Sometimes you can have everything in place but fall short because you just don't stick with it. Americans are notorious for this. I read a report that stated Americans get to about 85% of their goal, then lose interest and give up. This is not the case in Japanese culture, where they achieve 100%, then move on. Who is now the leader in many of the industries today? Persistence - stick-to-itiveness - is what makes all the difference in a person and an organization. Races, games, golf matches and life are won not by huge margins, but only by that little extra effort, that extra push that makes the biggest difference. I was watching the movie "Bull Durham" last night, and Kevin Costner was talking to the young pitcher who had just been called up to the major leagues. He stated that the only difference between someone with a batting average of 250 and a super star, with an average of 300, is just one more hit per week, but that one hit makes all of the difference in your career. If you are willing to put in the little extra bit of effort, to finish the task, to see the goal through to the end, it will make all of the difference in your career, your goals and the lives of those you lead.

"Victory belongs to the most persevering."

Napoleon

That's it. That's all there is to becoming a great leader among your peers. Just decide what it is that must be accomplished, communicate it to others, reward those who help in the effort, assume the role of the conductor and stick with it to completion, and your name will be written in the halls of leadership for eternity.

"The final test of a leader is that he leaves behind him in men the conviction to carry on."
Walter Lippmann

Vic Osteen

Vic Osteen has shared information on how to juggle the challenges of life without dropping the ball with audiences ranging from prisoners to presidents, speaking to associations and business audiences across the country.

Vic is a speaker, educator, author, horticulturist and entrepreneur. He has thrown newspapers, slung pizza, owned a plant store in the 70's, established 2 landscape companies and a lawn mower businesses. He has sold cow manure, sprayed lawns and is the director of marketing for Win Seminars.

He taught in the Oklahoma State Prison System for six years and has taught college and high school courses in management and marketing, as well as, a program Landscape and Golf Course Management. Vic has appeared on an NBC Television affiliate, as "Mr. Green Thumb", and a weekly radio call in program.

Vic holds a Degree in Horticulture-Floriculture / Retail Business, a Masters Degree in Trade and Industrial Education and is a Doctoral Candidate in Human Resource Development.

Through Growth Seminars his purpose is to teach people how to enjoy more productive, professional and personal lives. His entertaining presentations with a natural perspective provide solutions for better management, employee relations and personal development.

Programs Include:

The Design for Success
The steps to developing a life or business that will insure growth and happiness.

Tools for Teamwork - Growing A Better Workforce
Methods to turn your workforce into a motivated well oiled machine working together to produce a more enjoyable effective business..

A Legacy of Leadership -The Eleven Step Program to Excellence
How to develop leadership qualities in yourself and others.

Customer Service From The Ground Up
Methods that will help you grow your business through an attitude of service.

Juggling Your Time and Your Life
How to find all the time you will ever need and make every day count.

Other Products

Everything I Needed to Know I Learned in My Garden *- book* *$7.95*
161 lessons on life, relationship, and laughter learned from Mother Nature

Seeds of Hope *- quote book* *$10.00*
Quotes, poems, and thoughts of hope, success and happiness

Leaves of Leadership *- quote book* *$10.00*
Quotes to help you develop your own leadership style.

The E's of Successful Daily Living*-perpetual calendar* *$10.00*
31 E words, thought and quotes to keep you going through the year

The Design for Success *- Audio* *$10.00*
The plan for developing and living a life that you can love.

Only The Best On Customer Service*- book* *$11.95*
The best ideas on customer service in yourself and others from many of the same authors in this book.

Developing an Employee Manual *- workbook* *$35.00*
Produce your own employee manual with instructions, examples and work pages to help you produce a better business.

Timely Thoughts & Techniques *-62, 8.5 x 11 posters* *$10.95*
Colorful posters to keep you and others motivated and on target.

"Growth is the Key to Success, Plant the Planet" *T-shirt* *$20.00*
Cool 2 color T-Shirt with graphic to tell the world what you believe.

Please include $5.00 for shipping and handling
Mastercard and Visa Welcome.
For information on Vic's keynotes and seminars, please contact:

Growth Seminars
P.O. Box 52465
Tulsa, Oklahoma, 74152-0465
918/742-8454 • 800/746-8454 • Fax 918/747-3185

9

Only The **BEST**

The Art of Empowerment

"Leadership From The Inside Out"

By

Dan Clark

The Art of Empowerment

"Leadership From The Inside Out"

Dan Clark

Leadership is not a club or a title given to someone because of time spent or years of service rendered. Standing in the front of a room and calling ourselves a leader no more makes us a leader than standing in the middle of a garage makes us a truck! Leadership implies action - action from the inside out. True leadership is a performance-based, earned designation bestowed on those who exemplify passion and artistry in the three fundamental sources of success. Ironically, the three sources are best identified in the world of horse racing.

When a champion thoroughbred dies, they bury only three body parts that symbolize what it takes to be a champion: the <u>Head</u> for wisdom and will, the <u>Heart</u> for spirit and courage, and the <u>Hooves</u> for speed and efficiency. Champion leaders are champions because they also possess these same qualities. And because competent personal leadership is always requisite to effective organizational leadership, true leaders actively work to implement and assimilate these qualities into their everyday thoughts and actions. The natural consequence results in inspiring and empowering others to do the same.

THE SOURCE OF SUCCESS

HEAD

Wisdom and **Will** are found and perpetuated in three simple truths:

1) We cannot succeed alone. Each of us needs a "physical therapist of the mind and heart" to teach and inspire and stretch and push us to reach our full potential. In physical therapy we must stretch before we strengthen and the same holds true in sales, customer service, parenting, teaching, coaching, managing and leading. I know some intense individuals who push and stretch themselves to what they consider their limit, but this perceived limit is not their ultimate best. Sure, these individuals push themselves to the point of discomfort, but I know of no one who can push and stretch themselves beyond the point of discomfort without someone to help them reach further. Yet, it is in the zone past the point of discomfort where all the strengthening occurs. The sports cliché, "no pain no gain" is absolutely true in every aspect of living.

To succeed and become all we were born to be, we

need someone in our lives who sees us not just for who we are, but for who and what we have the potential to become. Someone who stretches us to the uncomfortable area beyond our comfort zone to a place we have never been before. When everyone else is running seven 50 yard windsprints for conditioning, this someone gets us to run three more. When everyone else is doing minimum work, reaching expected sales quotas and delivering expected customer satisfaction, this someone pushes and stretches us intellectually and emotionally to go beyond the expected to create sales records and extraordinary customer delight. Regardless of who we are, or the position we hold, we all need someone who will not let us settle for less than the very best. I call this special someone a "Wizard." And they are that "someone" not because they *understand* life, but because they *live* it. Sure, they practice what they preach, but more importantly, they preach only what they practice. This breeds love, respect, admiration, and an urgent willingness to let them push and stretch and lead us through their inspiring example. With an understanding that there are two ways to look at everything - eyesight and insight, a wizard leader unselfishly shares wisdom and will through simple but profound insights. Four of my favorite empowering wizardisms:

a) We are not paid by the hour, we are paid for the value we bring to that hour.
b) Pressure is not something that is naturally there. Pressure comes when you question your own ability. When

you know what you can do, there is never any question.

c) If you are not training and pushing yourself to your ultimate capacity and potential as a human being, someone else, somewhere else is. When you meet him, he will win.

d) It is easier to *act* your way into positive thinking than to think your way into positive action.

2) Attitude is the main thing. Validation of this truth comes as we deepen our definition. Using Numerology as our source for discovery, let us assign each letter of the word it's corresponding number from the 26 letters of the alphabet: A=1, T=20, T=20, I=9, T=20, U=21, D=4, and E=5.

A + T + T + I + T + U + D + E
1 + 20 + 20 + 9 + 20 + 21 + 4 + 5 =100%

Attitude equals 100%! Attitude means giving it 100% effort - giving it everything we've got when less would be sufficient. Most of us acknowledge this kind of effort with the overused proclamation "I did my best. All I can do is all I can do." An empowering wizard leader replies, "Great, but what if you are giving 100% effort to the wrong thing?" Have you ever wondered how an athletic team can practice three hours every day and never win a game? The only possible reasonable answer is they are giving 100% effort to the wrong things! They are confusing activity with accomplishment. They are putting in time, occupying space and achieving failure instead of getting desired results and success. Accomplishment comes when we understand that the main thing is to make the main thing the main thing. It comes when we focus on *what* is the right thing, *doing* the right thing, and doing it right the *first time.* As a wizard would say, "It's better to build a fence at the edge of the cliff than to park an ambulance at its base." Attitude is the main thing, the get-it-right-the-first-time fence of accomplishment. Remember, when your attitude is right, your abilities will always catch up!

3) Popular corporate culture says "It's all about team." Wrong! It's not all about team. Teams lose! It's about winning and WINNING has two "I's" in it. The first "I" represents Independent Individual Preparation - a commitment to personal *Character*, *Confidence* and *Consistency* in an ongoing welcoming environment of *Change.* The second "I" represents Interdependent Collaboration - a commitment to *Contribute our Time, Talents and Resources* for the benefit of all. Together, these two "I's" constitute the "Participation Paradigm" which empowers the team to win. The teams that win in the short term and especially in the long term, have the greatest number of individual "I's" on them, all sharing a collaborative organizational belief that "when the water in the lake goes up, all the boats rise with it." Corporations, Associations, Schools, and Families win and grow and continue to succeed only when their

individual members do. An organization is only as good as its people!

HEART

<u>**Spirit**</u> and <u>**Courage**</u> are found and perpetuated in two simple truths.

1. Mutual Respect and Support. The only place from which a person can grow is where he or she is. We are talking not just from the physical place, but more importantly, from the emotional place. The words *Mutual Respect and Support* suggest that wherever this place is, it is okay for you and for me to be. Okay because this is our current reality - our starting point of self discovery, self evaluation and self improvement. Okay because no matter what our past has been we have a spotless future. Okay because self is not discovered, self is created. When we acknowledge this, we come to grips with who we are and what we are not. And only when we understand this do we qualify to be a leader with the ability to reach out to whatever level others are working at and gently invite them to grow.

I realize this sounds reasonable and should be achievable, but society makes it difficult by putting too much emphasis on *"Having"* and not enough emphasis on *"Being."* Society makes it difficult to separate the person from the performance. We tend to judge one another's success by cars, clothes, summer cottages, and country club memberships. How shallow! We are all going to die, deal with it! Even the one with the most toys dies. What we need is direction on being fully alive!

J. Stone wrote: "The most visible creators are those artists whose medium is life itself. The ones who express the inexpressible without brush, hammer, clay or guitar. They neither paint nor sculpt. Their medium is being. Whatever their presence touches has increased life. They see and don't have to draw. They are the artists of being alive."

Artistry in living comes as we stop focusing on having fortune and fame and start focusing on being authentic and whole. When we identify ourselves in terms of what we do instead of who we are, we become a "human doing" instead of a "human being." This is unacceptable if real success and lasting happiness are what we seek. For this reason, we must assimilate this powerful, passionate principle of *Mutual Respect and Support* into our everyday lives. In doing this, we move the emphasis from "what" we do and place it on "why" we do it; we focus on purposes instead of just setting goals; we understand the differences between I Love You and I Need You; we push for and usually get commitment to excellence through unconditional love; we feel genuine acceptance and a spirited, supportive feeling of loyalty, team and togetherness; and we establish and perpetuate the most powerful respect and support principle of all — what goes around comes around.

2. Champions aren't great all the time, but they are great when they need to be. Emotion is the deciding factor and is vital to peak performance. We see it in nearly every game of professional basketball. They should just give each team 100 points and let them play the last two minutes of the game. Why? Because more happens in the last two minutes than happens in the rest of the entire game! Why? There is a spirit of urgency which creates emotion and courage to step up when the going gets tough. Emotion triggers endorphin release and adrenaline resulting in second wind, extra effort, and hustle. Hustle creates intense concentration and a finely tuned ability to focus on specific strategies and behaviors. This in turn breeds courage under stress, courage to play hurt and courage to never-say-never. It has been written "In the absence of emotion, there is no change." I agree. And because leadership is about change, we must figure out how to consistently create emotion during both on-task and off-task time. In the world of work, intelligence gets you the job, but it is *Emotion* that gets you the promotion! In the world of leadership, emotion is the primary human connector and requisite link between management and labor. It is the primary ingredient for inspiring and empowering others to be spirited, courageous, peak performers.

HOOVES

Speed and Efficiency are found and perpetuated in one simple truth:

Anticipation. Wayne Gretzsky was asked what single quality made him the greatest hockey player of all time. He answered, "Most players go to where the puck is. I go to where the puck is going to be." This means as leaders, we must begin with the end in mind. Perfecting the art of anticipation initiates this type of thinking and is critical to every success. Because every endeavor has three specific phases that we experience - the Pioneering stage, the Momentum stage, and the Restructuring stage - it is vital that we anticipate their impact and outcomes. Initially, they unfold in the order listed above but soon they mesh into simultaneous events. Pioneering is getting the wheels to turn - anticipating the obstacles, anticipating the capital needs. Pioneering is playing not-to-lose. The second stage, Momentum, is getting the wheels moving easier and faster and faster. It is overcoming the fear of failure which moves us from playing "not-to-lose," to "playing-to-win!" With every action, failure or success, we anticipate the next move. "What's next?" becomes our vocabulary for the day. Restructuring is the evaluation and processing of the momentum. It comes through anticipating change in economic and political direction, anticipating change in price and competition, and then responding appropriately. Restructuring is about being flexible and adaptable in every situation, making decisions based not on who's right, but on what's right.

Anticipation is critical throughout every phase of every endeavor - especially in leadership and empowerment. It is the powerful motivator that breeds speed and efficiency. Speed because you want the benefit now and efficiency because you don't want to waste any time getting it. Everybody wants to win, but very few people are willing to prepare to win. Helping others to anticipate keeps that preparation spark alive so they willingly pay the price today, enabling them to enjoy the prize forever!

Yes, the secret to empowering others and leading from the inside out is to fully utilize our Head, Heart and Hooves. True leadership is about Wisdom, Will, Spirit, Courage, Speed and Efficiency!

Dan Clark, CSP

Dan Clark, C.S.P. - Certified Speaking Professional, is one of the "hottest" speakers on the platform today. Since 1982, Dan has spoken to over two million people in all 50 states, throughout Canada, and in 11 other countries in Europe, Asia, and Russia.

Dan is the author of seven highly acclaimed books including "Getting High - How to Really Do It," "Puppies For Sale" (translated into Japanese and Russian), and "The Art of Being Alive." Dan is also a primary contributing author to the New York Times Best Sellers, "Chicken Soup for the Soul."

Dan is a successful businessman, actor, songwriter/recording artist, creator of over 40 audio and video training programs, and an award winning athlete who fought his way back from a paralyzing injury that cut short his football career.

Dan's client list is a Who's Who of the best organizations in the world including Meeting Professionals International, IBM, 3M, AT&T, Lucent Technologies, Boeing, ServiceMaster, Marriott Hotels, Nations Bank, Nordstrom, Prudential Insurance, Intermountain Health Care, Footlocker, the NCAA, the United Nations and hundreds more!

DAN CLARK, C.S.P.
Certified Speaking Professional
P.O. Box 8689
Salt Lake City, UT 84108

1-800-676-1121• 801-485-5755 • Fax 801-485-5789
Email sdanclarkp@aol.com

OTHER PRODUCTS

BOOKS

"The Art of Being Alive" .... $16.95 U.S.
(hard cover)
A parable revealing the 12 Precepts of the Art of Being Alive: Find a Mentor/Wizard, Live on Purpose, Create Mutual Respect and Support, Be True to Self, Keep Swinging, Communicate, Act-As-If, Increase Frequency of Feedback, Focus on Fundamentals, Expect Happiness, Manage Your Relationships and Follow the Final Formula. A must read book on Leadership, Empowerment and Personal Development relating to Management, Sales and Customer Service.

"Puppies For Sale" .... $12.95 U.S.
(soft cover - translated into Japanese and Russian)
This title comes from the tremendous popularity of one of Dan's many stories in the New York Times Best Sellers, "Chicken Soup For The Soul." This is Dan's own sequel collection of over 200 inspirational stories that will hug your heart and snuggle your soul. A perfect resource for speeches and articles.

"Getting High - How To Really Do It" .... $10.95U.S.
(soft cover)
Twelve chapters written especially for teenagers in language and stories they can understand. Motivation, Respect for Authority, Inspiration, Attitude, Goal Setting, Stay in School, Drug Prevention, Suicide Solution and Patriotism.

AUDIO TAPES

"The Art of Being Alive" .... $99.95 U.S.
A comprehensive series encompassing Dan's unique approach to life, personal and professional relationships, parenting, coaching and teaching. Dan discusses the 12 precepts of the Art of Being Alive. *12 audio cassettes recorded live with commentaries in the studio.*

"The Art of Relationship Management" .... $19.95 U.S.
Fundamental customer service concerns and advanced sales techniques that will give you the competitive advantage, increase sales, create customer delight, and positively effect your bottom line. *2 audio cassettes recorded live!*

"The Art of Empowerment" .... $19.95 U.S.
Effective leadership always comes from the inside out. Learn that control is only an illusion - learn the difference between inspiration and motivation, leadership and management; learn teambuilding skills from someone who actually played on a team; create a winning organization. *2 audio cassettes recorded live!*

"The Art of Teaching" .... $19.95 U.S.
Dan believes teaching is the profession that makes all other professions possible. A program especially for K-12 teachers, school support staff, secretaries, food service, transportation and custodians - everyone who is involved in the educational arena. *A 1½ hour in-service recorded live! 2 audio cassettes.*

Please included $5.00 U.S. shipping and handling • Mastercard and Visa welcome.
For a complete catalog of Dan's books, audio and video learning systems, music albums, t-shirts and posters, as well as information on Dan's keynote speeches and seminars, please contact Dan at:

Dan Clark & Associates
P.O. Box 8689 - Salt Lake City, UT 84108
1-800-676-1121, 801-485-5755, Fax 801-485-5789,
Email sdanclarkp@aol.com

10

Only The BEST

T^3: Top Ten Traits of Great Leadership

By

Shep Hyken

T^3: Top Ten Traits of Great Leadership

Shep Hyken

"You can create, design and build the most wonderful place in the world, but it takes people to make the dream a reality."
Walt Disney

Imagine you are sitting in a seminar and the speaker asks the audience to write down their definition of leadership. Then each of the seminar participants share their answers out loud. You wouldn't believe how many different answers you will hear! But, I have to believe that if Walt Disney was asked that question, he might very well have started with the above quote and finished by saying, *"and it is our leaders that will act as our guides and mentors to bring out the best in our people, so that our dreams really will come true."*

Today's great leaders are visionaries with very high values, who have the ability to persuade, teach, mentor, coach and move people to their highest levels of performance. These leaders aren't necessarily the CEO's and presidents of large companies and organizations. They may not even be in management. These great leaders are the ones within an organization that have the respect of their peers and the ability to do all of the above, regardless of position or job title.

The goal in this chapter is to give you a *Top Ten Traits* list of great leaders. This list is by no means complete, but just a start. Hopefully it is a catalyst to get you thinking about what traits you can add to the list. But, I will promise you this. The combination and use of these ten traits will move *your* leadership abilities to an even higher level.

1. Great leaders have character.

The essence of leadership is character. This includes integrity and honesty. First and foremost, a great leader must have respect and be admired as an honest, hard-working person by the people they work with. As soon as a leader's character is compromised, the respect of everyone working for him/her is lost. Character is the backbone of a great leader.

"You minus possessions equals character."
Anonymous

2. Great leaders don't do it alone.

A leader recognizes the abilities of others and empowers them. They realize that they can't do everything, and shouldn't try. In addition, a good leader never claims all of the credit. Instead, they pass it on to the people who really did the work. Unfortunately, many leaders fail in this area, and ultimately fail to gain trust and loyalty from the people they work with. In a recent issue of Fortune Magazine, Richard Hagberg, an executive development consultant, compiled a database of the characteristics of 511 CEO's using personality tests and evaluations from thousands of co-workers. Seventy percent of CEO's are considered loners, or as Hagberg says, "Rambo's in pin-stripes." Leaders that ultimately failed had oversized egos and were too independent with high needs for autonomy. They lacked the desire and sense to build strong, loyal relationships with their employees.

"The new leader no longer thrives on the glory of being first up the hill. In fact, he/she finds glory in the whole team reaching the summit together, then returning to camp to plan the victory celebration."

Bernard Nagle, Principal, LeaderCulture Resource

3. Great leaders make friends.

Great leaders' friendly relationships come from the respect and trust that they have for the people they work with. This cannot be developed overnight. It must be cultivated over time and comes from a sincere caring and respect for others . Great leaders have the ability to make people feel important at every level. Intimidation and fear are not part of their leadership tactics. When they walk the halls, employees do not cower in fear. Instead, they invite these leaders to share in their endeavors. A friendly business relationship builds loyalty.

"The reason we exist must surely be for each other."
Albert Einstein

4. Great leaders take responsibility.

As a leader, you and you alone are responsible for everything that those who follow you do, or fail to do. Hap Arnold was the five-star Commanding General of the Army Air Force during World War II and gives a crystal clear illustration of this point in his book, *Army Flyer*. A new squadron commander received a message from his group commander. "You drank too much at the Officer's Club last night. Don't let it happen again." The problem was that this young officer had never been at the Officer's Club on the night in question. Shrugging it off, he decided to do nothing. Several days later, he received another message. "You drank too much again. This is your final warning." The new squadron commander was really puzzled because he hadn't been at the club on that night either. This time, however, he called the deputy group commander to talk it over. The deputy group commander understood the situation perfectly. "Major, you're not responsible for just yourself anymore. You're now responsible for the actions of everyone in your squadron. You personally weren't drinking too much at the Officer's

Club. But one of the members of your squadron was, and you're responsible!"

"The buck stops here!"
Harry Truman

5. Great leaders are problem solvers.

Leaders not only solve problems, they have the ability to recognize them. One of the tests of leadership is the ability to recognize a problem before it becomes an emergency. There will always be fires to put out. The best leaders not only put them out, they learn from them. They look for the opportunity that problems present. Levi Strauss is a good example. He had the qualities of a leader and they literally took him from rags to riches. As a teenager he lived in Kentucky, working as a peddler. But when he heard about the *gold* in California, he felt compelled to head west. To earn money for his supplies, Strauss sold some of the merchandise he peddled to fellow passengers on his western trip. He sold everything but some rolls of tent canvas. Finally in San Francisco he was broke. All he had left was the unsold canvas. While in the marketplace he learned that there was a high demand for pants. Prospecting for gold was tough on pants. So, Levi Strauss found a tailor to make pants and overalls out of his canvas. He was so successful that he gave up the idea of prospecting for gold to make pants for the rest of his life.

"There comes a time in the affairs of man when he must take the bull by the tail and face the situation."
W. C. Fields

6. Great leaders are decision makers.

They aren't bogged down with the details. They leave the details to others and focus on the big picture. They have the ability to observe, process and move forward, and all of this without procrastination. You don't get to the top by wavering on issues and putting off important decisions. To the contrary, once a decision is made, a great leader will shift into forward gear.

"Decisiveness is not in itself a virtue. To decide not to decide is a decision; to fail to decide is a failure."
General George Patton

7. Great leaders know how to delegate and empower.

To delegate does not mean to empower. In most cases, employees have been delegated to a project with specific responsibilities, but not empowered to make important decisions without first having to ask someone, such as the "boss." The Ritz-Carlton hotel chain really does delegate and empower. The Ritz holds the satisfaction of the customer as sacred. They train every employee to take care of their specific job responsibility, but in addition, they are empowered to make sure that their customer satisfaction level is at its highest. For example, the housekeepers have the responsibility to clean the rooms and keep the hotel looking as great as always as well as being charged with the important responsibility of insuring the guest's satisfaction - the same as every other employee of the Ritz. If necessary, they have been empowered with the ability to spend up to $2,000.00 to insure the guest has been taken care of.

"The best leader is the one who has sense enough to pick good men to do what he wants done, and then the self-restraint to keep from meddling with them while they do it."
Theodore Roosevelt

8. Great leaders understand motivation.

This doesn't mean that great leaders possess abundant charisma, although it doesn't hurt! It simply means they understand how to motivate people. I've met some pretty boring CEO's of major organizations, but they know what gets people excited. They know the power and techniques of motivation and how to use them. Whether it be a pat on the back, a congratulatory note or an incentive program with elaborate awards, they understand what makes people tick. And, they do it.

"Our chief want in life is somebody who will make us do what we can."
Ralph Waldo Emerson

9. Great leaders show thanks.

A great leader will never miss an opportunity to show appreciation, even if it is just a simple thank you or a pat-on-the-back. They know the power of appreciation. It is a motivator and can even help to keep the best people. Recently, Robert Half International surveyed new employees of companies who had left their last job to make a lateral move. One would think that the number one reason might be more money. But, the number one reason employees jumped to another company was because they didn't feel appreciated by their employer. Great leaders know how important it is to show appreciation, and they do it.

"There is something that is much more scarce.
Something rarer than ability.
It is the ability to recognize ability."
Robert Half

10. Great leaders are learners.

A leader never passes up the opportunity to learn. They learn from the people they work with, industry experts, non-industry experts, seminars - the list goes on and on. In addition, great leaders are inspired by all of this learning. They tap into an endless source of ideas, knowledge, information, innovation and are compelled to action. They are proactive and aren't satisfied with merely sitting around and waiting for *stuff* to happen.

"Leadership does not happen from the fifty-second floor of the headquarters building. Leaders stay in touch. They stay in touch with trends in the marketplace. They stay in touch with the ideas and advice of others. They stay in touch with social, political, technological, economic and artistic changes. It is only by staying in touch with the world around them that leaders can ever expect to change the business-as-usual environment."

James Kouzes and Barry Posner, authors,
The Leadership Challenge

BONUS: Great leaders create Moments of Magic.

Walt Disney knew how to create magic at Disneyland a.k.a. the Magic Kingdom. It wasn't just one thing that did it. He took a number of important things and tied them together. He never compromised any of his standards and beliefs, for it would have taken away from the guest's magical experience. And, he inspired all of his people to this same level of thinking. His "cast members," as he called them, went through training and more training to learn and understand his philosophy. They were learning from the master. And, Walt Disney wasn't just barking orders from the helm. He walked the talk. He was part of it all. And that is what great leaders do. They have the ability to create *Disney Like Magic*, not just for their customers, but also for the people they work with and lead.

"Fools can learn from their own experience; the wise learn from the experience of others."
Democritus

And To Wrap All of This Up...

All of the above go into the making of a great leader. The *Top Ten Traits* discussed in this chapter are some of the secrets to unlocking the magic of great leadership. We all have what it takes. We just have to have the confidence and the ability to put them all together.

Shep Hyken

Shep Hyken, CSP is a speaker and author who has been entertaining audiences with his unique presentation style for 24 years. He has been hailed as one of the top entertainer/magicians working the corporate field. In 1983 he made the transition from entertainer to speaker. Hyken mixes information with entertainment (humor and magic) to create exciting programs for his audiences.

Shep Hyken has worked with hundreds of companies and associations ranging from "Fortune 500" size companies to smaller organizations with less than 50 employees. Some of his clients include American Airlines, Anheuser-Busch, AT&T, Fleming Foods, General Motors, Holiday Inn, Kraft, Monsanto, Shell Oil, Standard Oil and many, many more.

Main Topics Focus on:

Creating Moments of Magic, Excellent Customer Service, Customer Relations and Customer Retention — These presentations focus on how important service is in today's world. Make your organization a star in your customers' eyes. Some of the topics in these presentations include Jan Carlzon's Moments of Truth, Moments of Magic, parallels between selling and service, meeting and exceeding expectations, handling confrontations, building relationships and more.

Servicing Internal Customers — This is important to every employee of any business; from upper management to front line employees. Some of the areas discussed include the concept of the internal customer, management's new responsibilities and building better relationships. The front line may service, sell and have the most contact with the "outside" customer, but the internal people serve everyone else in the organization. Servicing and treating fellow employees like customers will have a direct positive effect on your organization's customer service/satisfaction program. Teamwork concepts can also be brought into this program.

You Are The Magic! — This motivational speech combines humor, magic, information and motivation to create an exciting and enlightening presentation for all types of audiences. It is a fun program that can incorporate parts of Shep's service programs or can include topics such as personal excellence, goal setting, turning negatives into positives, teamwork and more. This is an outstanding program for banquets and special events.

Focus On The Customer - LIVE! — Perhaps your organization has held focus groups where customers are brought into a comfortable environment and asked questions. Imagine taking the focus group live, in front of your organization's executives, sales people, etc. Shep Hyken will host and facilitate a focus group in front of your audience. Shep will learn specific information about your business and industry, learn about your customers, and develop questions to ask them. But most importantly, Shep will open the session up for questions from the audience. Your people will be able to ask these customers virtually any questions they have ever wanted to ask - no holds barred! Shep encourages participation and keeps the program moving with high energy and his own brand of humor. (You might say this is a cross between Phil Donahue and Jay Leno!)

OTHER PRODUCTS

Moments of Magic — 158 page book $12.95
A clearly written, easy-to-read, easy to understand guide to customer service for anyone in any job. It is filled with information, techniques, and stories that will teach you to deliver excellent service to your internal and outside customers.

The Winning Spirit — 198 page book $16.95
Published in cooperation with the United States Olympic Committee, twenty experts wrote on "achieving Olympic level performance in business and personal advancements." Authors include Shep Hyken (Gold Medal Customer Service), Frank Mcguire, Don Hutson, Tony Alessandra, Jim Tunney, Les Brown and more!

Only The Best On Success — 198 page book..................................... $11.95
If you like *Only the BEST On Leadership* you will love this book. Motivation and success are what this book is about featuring Shep Hyken writing on *You Are The Magic!* as well as other inspiring authors such as Roger Crawford, Mark Sanborn, Keith Harrell and more!

Only The Best On Customer Service — 226 page book $11.95
The third in the *Only the Best* series focuses on leadership and features Shep Hyken's chapter on *The Top Ten Traits of Great Leadership*. Other authors include Larry Winget, Scott McKain, Keith Harrell, Dan Clark, and more!

Shep Hyken "Live" on Customer Service — 55 minute video $49.00
This video on customer service covers topics such as complaining customers, relationship skills, moments of truth and other important issues. This was taped in front of a live audience and combines information and entertainment (humor and magic) to create an exciting presentation.

Service: Creating Moments of Magic — 2 videos & workbook $99.00
A video *learning system* with a focus on internal and external customers. The workbook includes exercises that will *personalize* the information to the viewer's day-to-day responsibilities. Additional workbooks are only $5.00 each. An outstanding tool!

Please add $4.00 Shipping & Handling
Mastercard and Visa accepted. Call regarding quantity discounts.

For more information on Shep's keynote presentations
and seminars, please contact:

Shep Hyken
Shepard Presentations
711 Old Ballas Rd., Suite 215 • St. Louis, MO 63141
(800) 829-3888 or (314) 692-2200 • FAX: (314) 692-2222
E Mail: ShepardH@aol.com
http://www.hyken.com/